MANAGING YOUR TAX SEASON

THIRD EDITION

EDWARD MENDLOWITZ, CPA/PFS/ABV/CFF/CITP, CGMA

15733-360

AICPA

Notice to Readers

Managing Your Tax Season, 3e does not represent an official position of the American Institute of Certified Public Accountants, and it is distributed with the understanding that the author and publisher are not rendering legal, accounting, or other professional services in the publication. If legal advice or other expert assistance is required, the services of a competent professional should be sought.

1 2 3 4 5 6 7 8 9 0 PIP 1 9 8 7 6 5 4

ISBN: 978-1-94165-130-8

Director, Content and Product Development: Linda Cohen
Acquisitions Editor: Erin Howard Valentine
Developmental Editor: David Cohen
Project Manager: Charlotte Ingles
Cover Design Direction: Nancy Karmadi

Acknowledgments

Many people deserve thanks for the preparation of this book. Some of them are acknowledged subsequently.

My partners at WithumSmith+Brown, P.C. (WS+B), especially Peter A. Weitsen who lived through many versions and experiments developing the techniques in our practice and who added many comments and ideas to this book.

Our clients, who were the targets of our desires to better serve them by creating greater efficiencies for their returns and the planning ideas behind the returns, which are the finished products of a continuous process.

My colleagues, including Ronald Bleich, Frank R. Boutillette, Ruben Cardona, Brian Lovett, John Mortenson, Shree Nadkarni, Joe Picone, Scott Perlzweig, Debra Schmelzer, Don Schneier, Howard Stein, Hal Terr, and MaryJane Younghans, who continually make suggestions and air ideas leading to smoother tax preparation processes. Special thanks to Bill Hagaman, the firm's managing partner, and Dave Springsteen, head of the tax department at WS+B, who keeps a close watch on our activities. All of them contributed ideas that are included in this book.

Other contributors to the preparation of this book include Martin Abo, Jake Ansel, E. Martin Davidoff, Donald R. Karlewicz, Michael Slotopolsky, Ronald B. Stricker and John Strydesky.

Thanks also to the AICPA Publications staff Erin Valentine and David Cohen. My son, Andy Mendlowitz, an author in his own right, who provided critical editing and comments.

Some of the material has been previously published in *How to Review Tax Returns* (CPA Trendlines 2014) by Edward Mendlowitz and Andrew D. Mendlowitz and I want to thank the publisher, Rick Telberg for permission to include it here.

My wife, Ronnie, who puts up with all the excess time I spend on my writing and my efforts to develop greater efficiencies in my practice, without whose love and support none of this would get done.

The following are practitioners who provided direction for, and reviews of, this book:

Louise H. Anderson, CPA
Davis, Monk & Company
Gainesville, Florida
Adele Brady Bolson, CPA, PS
(a member of the AICPA Private Companies Practice Section Executive Committee) Bellevue, Washington

Author's Note

Comments in this book make reference to my firm and how we do or did certain steps or procedures. The procedures include what was done in Mendlowitz Weitsen LLP, before it was merged into WithumSmith+Brown; procedures at WithumSmith+Brown; and procedures adopted from firms that were acquired and merged into our practices either before or after we merged with WithumSmith+Brown. However, all opinions and comments are mine, and no endorsement or acknowledgment should be inferred from the personal mention of my firm's procedures.

Contents

About the Author

Edward Mendlowitz, CPA, PFS, ABV, CFF, CITP, CGMA is partner emeritus in the CPA firm WithumSmith+Brown, P.C., located in New Brunswick, N.J. He is a member of the AICPA, the New Jersey Society of Certified Public Accountants (NJSCPA), and the New York State Society of CPAs (NYSSCPA). Currently, he is on the NYSSCPA Estate Planning Committee, and previously, he was the chairman of the committee that planned the NYSSCPA's 100th anniversary. Mendlowitz has authored 23 books and edited 6 others, has written hundreds of articles for business and professional journals and newsletters, and has written and presented over 200 different continuing education programs for CPAs. He is a contributing editor to PPC's *1998/1999 706/709 Deskbook, The Corporate Controller's Handbook of Financial Management, Wiley's Handbook on Budgeting* and the AICPA's *Management of an Accounting Practice Handbook*. He is on the editorial board of *BottomLine/Personal* newsletter. He appears regularly on television news programs, and his practice management techniques have been reported on by many publications, including *The Wall Street Journal*, the *Journal of Accountancy*, and *Practical Accountant*. He is the winner of the Lawler Award for the best article published during 2001 in the *Journal of Accountancy*. He also taught in the MBA graduate program at Fairleigh Dickinson University and is admitted to practice before the United States Tax Court. He has been qualified as a team captain and has performed peer and quality reviews of CPA firms.

Mendlowitz has spoken on practice management for the AICPA and the New York, New Jersey, and Connecticut State Societies of CPAs, as well as many other professional accounting groups. His *Managing Your Tax Season* program has been the most popular NJSCPA management of an accounting practice program, with over 30 presentations since 1980. He is also a consultant to a number of CPA firms. Mr. Mendlowitz is the president of the WS+B Partners' Network which offers practice management support to over 1,000 smaller CPA practices.

Mendlowitz is the author of a twice-a-week blog that discusses issues clients have expressed interest in: www.partners-network.com. Mendlowitz can be reached at WithumSmith+Brown, P.C., One Spring Street, New Brunswick, NJ 08901; telephone: 1-732-964-9329; fax: 1-732-964-9330; e-mail: emendlowitz@withum.com. Do not hesitate to contact the author to discuss anything in this book or to request Microsoft Word or Excel files of information discussed.

Updates and additional information can be viewed at the author's personal website: www.edwardmendlowitz.com.

Introduction

Tax season does not end on April 15. Tax preparation and tax planning have become a year-round service. There is really no time anymore that can be called purely tax season.

Tax season is a continuous process because of the impossibility of CPA firms preparing all the returns that need to be completed by April 15. Most (almost all) firms prepare returns and are heavily involved in their individual tax practice and client interaction 12 months a year.

This book has been prepared to help tax practitioners better serve their clients by using more effective processes and procedures in the office throughout tax season.

Tax season is a high-stress time. Systems need to be established that ease the tension and allow time not only to be thoughtful and consider the issues for return preparation but also to uncover and develop tax and financial planning opportunities for your clients.

The point of managing a tax season is that each accountant has a system. It may not be as good as it could be, but it is a system that works for that practitioner. This book helps you recognize that you have such a system and shows you ways to improve it, streamline it, or amend it, so that tax season will be less burdensome and more profitable.

Tax season starts October 16—the day after the final extensions are due—and ends the following October 15. Then, it restarts. To simplify the presentation of the material in this book, I have broken this year-round process into firm preparation and return preparation. These preparations are no less complicated than the most involved projects and require management as intricate as does any essential service. Your goal in the year-round process is to create a world-class tax department.

A world-class tax department provides great service to every client, user-friendly services, responsiveness to client questions and ideas, creativity as well as precision, and the ability to anticipate client concerns. This department also has interested, interesting, and excited people working in an environment that fosters everything a world-class tax department should do.

A world-class tax department only has "A" clients, and treats people who would be someone else's "B" or "C" clients as "A" clients. The difference is that the world-class tax department assigns the proper level of staff to clients so each receives world-class treatment.

User-friendly services are standard in a world-class tax department. This department recognizes that its job is to communicate what it does so the desired actions will result. That communication can be achieved only when clients are fully interactive in the process, which means employing completely user-friendly methods.

Responsiveness to client questions and ideas is also critical to a world-class tax department. However, responsiveness is more than good business, it is also common courtesy. A good way to provide optimal responsiveness is to picture yourself as the client and imagine what you expect—and then do better.

A world-class tax department requires creativity as well as precision. Tax practitioners must be able to apply the full scope of their knowledge to every situation, juxtaposing tax law and rulings and cases and fact patterns and reasoning so they can recommend the best course for the client.

Anticipating client concerns is de rigueur in a world-class tax department. Its tax planners recognize that clients ask questions and express ideas in the context that they understand within the scope of their knowledge and experience. The planner must be able to flush out the real reason for the question or concern and must not be afraid of asking multiple questions to make sure that he or she truly understands the client. A world-class tax planner cannot be embarrassed to give simple solutions to complex questions, if that is what is required, and such a planner should not be afraid to say "No" to a client if doing so is in the client's best interest. These planners have to be well rounded and involved in more than just taxes and the tasks they work on; they have to bring an insatiable curiosity, inquisitiveness, and worldliness to the table. They also have to be able to integrate real-world situations and patterns into the client's proposed transactions. A world-class tax planner has to recognize that each day, client, and question present new opportunities, and he or she has to look at these new opportunities as exciting.

World-class tax department personnel have to be interested in, and excited about, what they do, and they must be able to infectiously convey that interest and excitement. Having a world-class tax department is a continuum of activities. There is no conclusion to a discussion on running a world-class tax department—only a series of beginnings.

SECTION I

Firm Preparation: Firm Retrospective and Business Model 1

In many respects, there is a major beneficial side effect to tax season. The sharp concentration of work creates the need for innovation and quick training to lessen the time spent on tax preparation and eases the workload. This need has led firms to hire temporary seasonal help; use service bureaus to outsource their tax return processing or parts of it; purchase in-house computer systems, high-speed laser copiers, scanners for digitization, smart scanners to populate tax programs, paperless procedures; secure portals and storage, mobility and swift adaptation to cloud-based software. In a lot of respects, smaller firms led the way with technology because they were forced to look for innovative methods and were able to make the quick acquisition decisions that the tax season demanded.

The tax preparation portion of your practice is a separate business, and it needs continuous product development, work efficiency improvement, and service program upgrades. Issues for a firm to focus on annually include the following:

- Conducting a retrospective to determine whether there will be any systemic changes either firm-wide or limited to the tax season department procedures (chapter 1).
- Considering all the options available to the firm for managing seasonality. This may include reconsidering options that were rejected the previous year (chapter 2).
- Updating tax materials, including tax handbooks for staff and forms for the new year, plus an update and installation of tax preparation software and considering moving to the Cloud (chapter 3).
- Identifying clients who will need pre-year-end planning and tax projections. Calls are made to obtain their most recent tax information; then, appointments, when appropriate, are made to meet with the clients (chapter 4).
- Preparing mailings to clients, which include a year-end tax planning newsletter to be mailed out before the end of November

and organizers to be mailed (or emailed) in the middle of January (chapter 5).

- Implementing a staff tax training program, which includes an end of January or early February pre-tax-season staff meeting (chapter 6).
- Updating tax client lists and preparing preliminary staff assignment schedules (chapter 7).
- Reviewing staff hours and payment arrangements and communicating to staff at the staff meeting (chapter 8).

Review and procedure evaluations have to be conducted frequently and carefully to determine how to make the process better. In particular, at the end of tax season, when it is fresh in everyone's mind, the firm should review how the season went. This includes reviewing the firm's structure and processes, which are discussed in the following sections.

The results of both analysis and suggestions for improvement are outlined in a memorandum by staff level personnel. This memorandum is distributed before the retrospective meeting.

Structure

As in any department of an accounting firm, there must be an organization structure. Typically, a partner heads the tax department.

Tax services for clients are a complicated function, and its intricacies are often overlooked or unappreciated by clients and, sometimes, the CPA firm partners and staff. Taxes are subdivided into many separate specialties—preparation, compliance, research, projections, and planning—with each specialty further subdivided. For example, the tax return preparation process is separated into meeting with the client, compiling and assembling the information, preparing the return, perhaps researching some issues, reviewing the return, communicating the results to the client, and planning and projecting for the current year and future years.

The hard part of planning and ensuring that everyone is properly oriented is to recognize the differences and then to prepare accordingly by making sure everyone is coordinated. We find that separating the functions makes tax season flow much more smoothly. Even smaller firms can benefit from this.

Usually higher- or partner-level people interview the clients and get their information. They have to develop a method of taking notes and writing instructions and comments that are easy to read (in my case, decipher) and follow.

Lower-level staff prepare the returns, but they need a resource person to go to for assistance, direction, and guidance; that person must be available to help them or bottlenecks (and unhappy staff and clients) will result.

In most firms, the staff is segmented into service categories, with the bulk of the staff working on audits, financial statement preparation, or recurring work. Tax returns, being extra work, are added to the corporate and business return work, which is also extra work but part of the firm's base of services. Accordingly, every person in the firm has to be conscripted to work on tax returns, either to prepare or review. Ideally, a firm would have a permanent tax preparation department, but the workload is not spread evenly throughout the year, so most firms cannot do this. Using part timers, per diem people, outsourcing and careful and smart scheduling also helps manage the workload. Tax season is a time when everyone needs to participate, especially during the crunch time: the last week in March and first week or two in April. A by-product of the tax season preparation is that the staff becomes well rounded and tax knowledgeable.

Higher-level staff have to review the returns. Also, procedures, which will be discussed later in this publication, have to be put in place to reduce the review time; otherwise, bottlenecks will result here.

Partners and client contact managers have to be available to make decisions and advise clients of the returns' progress.

In the retrospective, a firm needs to identify any bottlenecks that occurred due to structure and consider adjustments to eliminate or minimize them in the upcoming tax season.

Processes

Tax season is a microcosm of everything done in an accounting practice. One of the primary concerns of a business is having proper processes and quality control procedures. Because of the compression of work in a relatively short period, tax season provides an excellent opportunity for a continuous quality control initiative, the goal of which is reducing errors and increasing planning. Irrespective of the crush of work and deadlines, whenever a systemic or repetitive error is uncovered, you should look at that as the time to find the cause and then institute whatever procedures you can that will eliminate such errors in the future. We did, and one of our results was to reduce by half the tax notices our clients receive. This effort has also led to many other time-saving initiatives, which are accomplished by analyzing tax return review notes and tax notices. Even though you are swamped, you should take the time for process improvement as the situation arises or you will never achieve the growth you might desire.

Tax Return and Financial Statement Review Notes

Copies of all tax return and financial statement review notes are collected and analyzed to determine the types, categories, and repetition of errors and changes to the returns and reports; who is making the errors; and the progress made to reduce the incidence of errors. An example of the types of items that might reoccur would be shareholder loan issues or personal auto use.

The object of this analysis is to raise the service level to clients, their confidence in the firm, and their overall financial security by providing error-free work to them. This will also make the firm's staff prouder and more confident in what they do, as well as more responsible for their work and more aware of the errors' costs.

With regard to review notes, I do not recommend retaining them beyond tax season or for the short period afterwards where they are used to increase quality and possibly change procedures. The notes primarily have notations about errors. There is no reason to keep work product that is discoverable in litigation. However, I would keep the preparer and reviewer checklists which are part of and evidence of your quality control system.

Tax Notices

A review is also made of tax notices received during the last year, what the notices were for, and who worked on the returns that generated the notices. The purpose is to determine if there are patterns to the notices, or the person who prepared the return, or if there is an absence of notices for returns prepared by some and a deluge for returns done by others. The firm most definitely needs to find out about any absence of notices so it can replicate what those staff members are doing. The firm should also try to monitor client complaints and compliments.

In that regard, our monitoring showed that a major source of notices has been for erroneous reporting of estimated tax payments. Most of the time, the errors are due to incorrect information the client provides to the firm. Accordingly, one solution is to require clients to provide proof of payment when they submit their tax information. Everyone working on returns should get that information.

In many cases, slightly more deliberate thinking about what is being done, its purpose, and the expected or intended reaction or response of the client will reduce the errors. In others, a less rushed attitude will do the job. And in still others, a little extra attention to the final product works.

Types of Changes

Be aware of this program for what it is: a tool to try to identify areas where service to clients and firm efficiency could be improved. This program should not be thought of as a method of eliminating every mistake. The freedom to make mistakes could create an environment that, at the proper time, will encourage initiative, imagination, and a degree of aggressiveness in representing clients' best interests. Also, be mindful that if an associate does not ever make errors, this behavior might indicate a passivity that would cause the firm to not represent clients as fully as it should.

Keep in mind that the search is for patterns rather than isolated instances. The object is to reduce carelessness and inattention to what is being done, as well as to improve the efficiency in the way the staff work.

Some of the procedural changes we made or instituted because of this program are as follows:

- Signed copies of all engagement letters will be given to our administrative assistant, who will enter the appropriate information in the Tax Control. This was a result of information not being entered in the Tax Control for new engagements that grew out of initial single-purpose noncompliance jobs. We also now require engagement letters for all assignments, with the exception of individual tax return preparation (which we should insist on, but do not).

- If a staff person wants to do something that will take more than one hour, he or she must first clear it with a partner. Previously, staff who were frequently interrupted by so-called "urgent requests" by clients and who decided to work on those requests determined that the new request was of a greater priority than what they are working on. That's changed.
- All requests for tax research must now be in writing, with an estimated time limit for the research and due date. This requirement will force the requestors to be more careful and selective in their request and will clarify and possibly limit the issues and questions to be addressed.
- Many of the errors were because the checklists were not properly or completely filled out. Some of the errors were due to carelessness, but because the errors were widespread, we have changed our training to emphasize adherence to the procedures and attention to the questions. Some of the omissions are "non-number" items, such as the clients' telephone numbers and birthdates of the clients and their children.

Why Checklists Are Critical

> *Author's Note: This is an area I feel very strongly about, and it is a major reason for the success of the better firms and the lack of growth of smaller firms. Please read this section carefully and do not hesitate to call me with any questions about using checklists.*

By my way of thinking, a system must be established to assure the greatest quality at every level, reduce the number of touches per return, and present the client with the type of return with the right degree of planning he or she is relying on you to deliver. This system is the strict adherence to the processes and procedures, and it includes the careful and deliberate use of checklists.

Following are some bullet points that will explain what I believe and want to convey to you:

- Delegating means leveraging work, which creates opportunities for the delegator and delegate.
- Opportunities for the delegator and delegatee mean professional growth in a planned, organized manner.
- Delegating means trusting that what is needed to be done will be done the way it needs to be done.
- Firm systems create a method of training, supervision, oversight, and confidence that the work will be done the way it needs to be done.
- The system makes it easier to delegate and manage because a structure is in place.
- Checklists are part of the system and make it easier to lay out what needs to be done and how it should be done and in what order.
- Not doing the checklists the right way cancels everything I just said and creates added work and the need for supervision.
- Not doing the checklists also reduces profits; remember that you are running a business.

Checklists

Most people do not like filling out checklists. Why? I don't know because I like them.

Checklists create order, cause me to not reinvent the wheel every time I need to do something I previously did, create a place where I can list things that need to be done that won't be forgotten, help me make sure I cover everything I am supposed to cover, and enable me to more easily pass on what I know and have learned from my experiences.

Checklists also make it easier to assure the quality of work and procedures of people I supervise. Despite these many benefits, many staff members do not like to fill them out, including both less- and more-experienced staff and even some partners.

The issue with many checklists—and this is especially so with income tax preparation—is that the checklists are just too long. The AICPA Tax Section checklists and PPC Tax Preparation checklists run over 20 pages; however, in these instances there is a very good reason for their length. Tax returns are very complicated, requiring a myriad range of knowledge that most preparers, many reviewers, and few partners possess.

Many firms try to solve this problem by abandoning checklists or circumventing them by preparing their own one-page checklist. Some firms even look the other way, knowing the completed checklists were not read. In my opinion, these acts destroy your quality control system.

Tax returns take time. At many firms, the newer staff (read that as less experienced) prepare returns. In some firms, very experienced audit staff take time off from their audits to prepare or, worse, review returns. That quality must be assured is a given, yet procedures are followed that cause reduced quality, a poor result, greater overall time spent on the returns, greater time spent by overstressed reviewers, and less profits.

Zero Tolerance

If it were up to me, I would have a zero tolerance policy for noncompliance with checklists and procedures. If firm partners take the time and expend the effort to develop standardized forms and checklists, they should also commit to having these procedures followed. I find that many firms have great systems in place but that they don't follow through on the implementation and actual use. This is a defect of management and shows a lack of leadership. It also shows me a firm that is not maximizing its potential for profits. Isn't that why you are in business?

Smaller Firms

I continually get emails and calls from smaller firms including one-owner practices with one or two staff questioning the value of what I said and suggested in the previous two editions of this book. Many of these procedures started when I was moonlighting and evolved into procedures and processes that I used as my practice grew and that I still recommend today. Almost everything in this book can be adapted by the smallest firm as well as the largest. Actually, the smaller firms can introduce new processes easier and quicker than larger firms where anything new needs to get sign-off from multiple partners and layers of management. Here is one example to illustrate my point about applicability to smaller practices: I prepare my own return and no one reviews it for me. By using the Excel tax comparison worksheet, I am able to perform an effective self-review and catch any errors I've made before I file the return. In larger firms where many times there is a disconnect between the partner and the preparation of the return, the Excel tax comparison worksheet serves the function of allowing the partner to get the big picture of the client's previous year income and expenses in comparison to the last two or three years' returns, make sure all categories are covered (such as real estate taxes and mortgage interest), get some ideas for planning (such as a SEP or 401(k) for a self-employed client), that the return has been properly prepared, and that the client could understand the information on the return by looking at or having the partner review the return with the client, by going over the Excel sheet, all in a minute or two. A smaller practice can introduce the Excel sheet as a procedure quite easily; a larger firm cannot. There are many other illustrations, but the point is that everything in here is relevant for any size firm and smaller firms should not prejudice themselves before considering how these ideas might work for their firm. Also, I welcome emails and calls from readers. Send me an email with your question and include your phone number and I'll likely call you to discuss your question or issue, or email you something I've written elsewhere addressing your question.

Individual Tax Preparation Pre Hand-in for Review Procedure Sample Checklist

The following checklist is not a tax preparation checklist but a checklist of some essential steps that a preparer must do before handing in a return to be reviewed.

Sample

Individual Tax Preparation Pre Hand-in for Review Procedure Checklist

(Please fill this out only after you have completed each of the steps below)

Taxpayer:

Preparer:

Initial when complete:

1. Look at and compare to last year's tax return.
2. Look in paperless filing cabinet for any information received during the year that is needed for current year return.
3. Make sure all questions were resolved and all missing information was obtained.
4. Prepare the tax payments worksheet and the Schedule D reconciliation worksheet and scan into working papers with the tax work papers.
5. Review the completed return in Print Preview, including Diagnostics.
6. Look at two year comparison (or Excel tax comparison worksheet if applicable).
7. Clear all diagnostics and E-filing rejects.
8. Make sure that the last thing that you do is a full recompute and create the electronic file.

Please include this checklist on the outside of the client's documents when you route them to review.

Consider Options for Managing Seasonality 2

Tax season creates terrible workflow issues in accounting firms.

The work for year-end business client financial statements is always bunched up in the first quarter of the year. Added to this are the tax returns for business clients and then comes the influx of once-a-year tax-return clients (both business and individual returns).

Part of the added time needed can be made up with night and week-end work. However, the deadline pressures and sheer volume make work during tax season burdens for even the heartiest of us.

Managing seasonality has universal elements, although there is no set formula. Every firm seems to think it has unique ways to deal with seasonality. Each firm tries and tries and tries and still ends up with the same bunching and crunching under the worst conditions that professionals can work under—there is just too much work to do in a short period of time.

Seasonality requires determining the peak periods and then scheduling the staff appropriately. Some firms impose mandatory excess night and weekend hours and others keep the evening work to a minimum until the real crunch starts, and then ask for extra hours almost every night during the busiest periods.

Another thing is to be realistic about the seasonality of our business. Work not done during tax season will have to be done at some point. Tax preparation is always extra work, and unless there is a dedicated year-round staff for it, it will always be fill-in or after-hours work. In most practices, chargeable hours are always lower in the summer months because of vacations and many people working shorter weeks, not because of its being a slower time. These practices' shorthandedness during the summer doesn't leave time to complete their tax preparation. Meanwhile, September is a busy month because of the corporate and partnership tax extension deadline and the start of work on the extended individual returns. Also, staff spend some excess (and wasted) time on the September individual estimated tax payment amounts if they have not yet completed returns that were extended, or if they did not have the foresight to prepare the estimated vouchers through September when they prepared the extensions in April.

January is usually a busy month that requires overtime because of year-end fiscal year closings. Also, many smaller firms that prepare after-the-fact payroll taxes commit a lot of time to W-2 preparation and the other year-end payroll forms. One method of reducing time is to outsource the work to a payroll preparation firm, such as Paychex or ADP (but then the revenue is forfeited).

Short of declining to prepare tax returns for nonbusiness clients, creative and imaginative methods have to be used to reduce the bottleneck and work overload.

Firm plans to deal with seasonality have to be balanced against the need to get the work done timely, correctly, efficiently, and profitably. Some options for firms to consider include the following:

- Use extensions liberally to stretch out the preparation of tax returns throughout the year.
- Hire extra staff and temporary and per diem help.
- Facilitate telecommuting.
- Outsource preparation to off-site domestic vendors and offshore places.
- Aggressively use digitalization and technology to reduce the time spent preparing returns.
- Designate specific times when individual returns must be worked on.
- Do not accept new individual tax clients.
- Impose deadlines for receipt of information after which returns will be put on extension
- Evaluate existing clients.

Extensions

Extensions are a way to even out the workflow. However, once extensions are filed, the likelihood is low that the return will be looked at before mid-May. Also, unless the firm has a dedicated tax preparation staff, the preparation work will not get done efficiently because night and weekend work will be nonexistent. With summer vacations, the firm will be shorthanded throughout July and August because those working will be filling in for the vacationers. This brings the extended returns to September and early October.

The solution is to get as many returns as possible done during tax season. Also, it takes time (and many times, unrecoverable time) to prepare extensions. Filing on time will eliminate that excessive time or rather add that time to the productive preparation of the returns that would have been extended.

Seasonal Staff

The demands of tax season, including the compression of an unbelievable volume of work into a short period, require novel ways to get the work done. One such way is to hire seasonal or per diem preparers. It seems highly skilled people are available for tax season at reasonable rates. One positive aspect of tax preparation is that much of the work and process is high volume, modular, and repetitive, making it easier to teach. Per diem personnel can work either on a seasonal basis or year round.

One potential problem with temporary people is controlling the quality of their work. Part of this is their ability to fit in and adapt to the systems and processes that make everyone able to work together as a team, rather than separate people under the same roof.

Not considered in the category of seasonal staff are summer interns who also can work during tax season. This is a very easy way to introduce bright college students to the firm and for the firm to get a good look at them. Interns can be trained in preparing the more tedious parts of the returns, with the more responsive interns learning the entire returns. With the right training, the interns can become productive very quickly.

Determining tax season hours for seasonal staff and interns is very simple. When and how many hours they want to work is okay. Each person has his or her own schedule and personal time requirements.

Telecommuters

Using technology effectively can also allow people to work at home when they cannot, for personal or family reasons, be in the office. A parent who has to stay home with a sick child can now do a day's work by telecommuting, when in the past, a day or more of work would have been lost.

While at one time, many firms only permitted telecommuting under special personal circumstances, this work arrangement has become much more widespread, with some staff regularly telecommuting rather than working in their offices every day. Some firms are reducing private office areas and replacing them with common area desks with docking stations, eliminating some fixed office costs. With secure virtual personal networks and other remote access cloud-based programs and high-speed Internet access, people can work at home and have the same ability to use the software and paperless filing cabinets as they would if they were sitting in the office.

Telecommuting would be useful and practical with seasoned per diem people who are used to working on their own and who work on smaller, high-volume returns that would also need minimal review time. The information can be scanned in the office and e-mailed to them; they can work on the returns and e-mail them back. This is not much different from the outsourcing processes described in the next section.

Outsource

Many firms are starting to outsource their return preparation. The results have been mixed, but many firms who outsourced are repeating the process and increasing the returns done in this manner.

In evaluating an outsourced firm, your due diligence should be similar to that when hiring staff—check references, question them, find out about their quality control and internal control procedures, get assurances of their security processes, check professional accreditations, find out employee qualifications, and inquire into the firm's financial viability. I would not want to be the first customer of a newly formed firm.

The clients chosen for outsourcing should be carefully selected. You would have to consider the business aspects if a client objected to it after the fact and consider the feelings of the clients selected. The availability and use of outsourcing has to be balanced against not being able to get the returns done on time.

With regard to outsourcing, although the physical return might be done out of the office, the analysis, tax and financial planning, and review are done in the CPA's office. The creative and innovative part of tax return preparation is still done there—it is not outsourced and cannot be outsourced because it is our core activity. Typically, rules-based work can be outsourced, but the judgment-based work is retained. The face-to-face relationship, telephone calls, and client interaction remain in the accountant's office.

To send a return to the outsource provider, the client's information must be scanned and e-mailed or sent by secure portal to the processing center. The original documents would be returned to the client in a nice neat package.

The return is prepared and sent by e-mail to be reviewed in your office. The review time should be no more than if the return were prepared in your office, except that the reviewer has to be prepared to make the necessary changes, rather than give the return back to the original preparer. In fact, the return can be reviewed by an in-office preparer before it is turned in to the review department.

Following is a brief calculation of the cost and benefits of outsourcing returns. The first illustration is for a fairly basic return. The second illustration is for a rather complex return.

	Illustration 1	**Illustration 2**
Cost per return	$ 75.00	$ 75.00
Number of returns outsourced	50	50
Total cost	$3,750.00	$3,750.00
Hours saved per return	2	4
Total hours saved	100	200

(continued)

	Illustration 1	Illustration 2
Number of hours in a day	8	8
Number of days saved	12.5	25
Cost per hour saved	$ 37.50	$ 18.75

The cost per hour saved is significant only if it is equal to or less than the cost per hour you would have incurred. If you are paying under $18.75 per hour in illustration 2 or less than $37.50 per hour in illustration 1, there would be no cost benefit.

However, the cost saved might not be as meaningful as the time saved. Saving approximately 12.5 or 25 workdays from the 2- or 2.5-month tax season period is quite substantial when considering that an extra person to supply those days might not be available, and if such person were available, there would be extra tumult and traffic and interruptions in the office with the additional person, as well as extra costs, such as desk space, paper handling, telephone usage, coffee or sodas, and lunches or dinners.

The turnaround period of about three days is no longer, and probably shorter, than if the return were done in your office with per diem help.

Another saving would be the time to prepare extensions for returns that could not get done on time. This time is "lost"; unrecoverable; and, in most cases, not billable.

Privacy issues have been raised, but we don't believe a client's privacy is violated. Also, firewall security is built into the system. Sending returns domestically over the Internet creates breaks in security or confidentiality if someone were inclined to break into your or your clients' servers. We know of the NSA's system being broken into and there have been reports of the Israeli Secret Intelligence Service's computer system being broken into and confidential data extracted. If it could happen to them, we think there can be no completely safe system, internal or external.

If you send returns out of the United States, you must address client disclosure issues before deciding to do returns this way.

Smart scanning and scan and populate software is another form of outsourcing and is becoming more popular. Regardless of any supposed objections, I feel that it must be tested or given a try. Every firm I know that is using this method speaks highly of it and each year expands it use.

Technology

Our firm has adopted a completely paperless tax season. All file copies are maintained in a paperless environment. Almost all of the returns we prepare are filed electronically, and we use a portal to deliver returns to clients. We no longer e-mail clients' copies in PDF format. As mentioned previously, smart scanning is used for almost all of our returns.

Technology is a primary driver of a successful tax season. Older and slower equipment could cost up to 1 hour per day, reducing productivity by 12 percent to 15 percent. Necessary equipment will be computers, high-speed scanners, smart scanners and second and third monitors. For those working at home, portable high-speed scanners and monitors are standard. Also helpful will be networked high-speed printers and, possibly, personal printers. Your Internet access lines should be fast and able to handle portal transmission and downloading or upgrading tax software unless you use cloud-based software which I believe many smaller practices do not. Upgrading before tax season could bring back most of your costs by the end of tax season. Using the latest non tax program software is also necessary, though it is almost impossible not to.

Designated Time for Individual Tax Returns

Designating a time for tax return preparation is a very important part of tax season. For most firms, tax preparation is added or extra work. Because of this, the regular work continues and usually takes precedence. Regular, time-sensitive work can include continuously serviced clients; annual audits and other financial statement work needed for credit and shareholder purposes; or the life cycle work that needs immediate attention by the accountant, such as a divorce investigation or valuation for an estate or a client transaction.

Accordingly, if the tax season work is not scheduled or allowed for, it simply won't get done. For that reason, certain blocks of time need to be specially designated as "tax preparation time." This could be one or two nights per week or certain weekends and certain weekdays. At those times or on those days, everyone must work on individual tax returns or tax season work. This method guarantees that adequate time is spent on the tax work.

One way of assigning or permitting tax season overtime is to consider whether that staff accountant would have worked those nights or weekend days to do the nontax season work they were going to do if it were July instead of March. If he or she would have worked those hours in July, then he or she would be excused from the tax season work for those hours.

Another benefit of specially designated time is that when everyone is working on the tax season work, peer people are available to assist with questions and issues, rather than going to higher-level people.

New Clients and Latecomers

The firm should try to control the flow of work by the way the client interviews done to obtain tax information are scheduled and the procedure of accepting new clients late in tax season.

Many times, clients who come late only do so because they are not asked to come earlier—or are not contacted at all—and they "wake up" at the end of the first week in April. If we have the information, we try to complete the return. The bottleneck during the last week of tax season is not in the preparation but in the review and return processing. If the return is not done by April 15, chances are it won't get done until September.

Accepting new clients is a business decision that should be made on a client-by-client basis. The referral source, type of return, fee to be charged and staffing are all factors that need to be considered. I do not suggest a blanket policy. We have gotten some very good business clients through new tax clients that came in the second week in April. One thing we are very clear about is the fee we will charge for the return. Many last-minute clients are looking for an upgrade to the tax preparation service they used last year but do not understand that upgraded services suggest upgraded fees.

Existing Clients

Handling seasonality involves evaluating your clients to determine if they are appropriate for your practice, to see that they don't stretch your resources, and to ensure that they are profitable. Problem clients can be dropped. How problem clients are defined is very subjective and varies from firm to firm. Examples of problem clients could be those who

- send in their tax information piecemeal or don't provide all the data and then expect the preparer to make up the missing pieces.
- call constantly to find out how much progress has been made.
- come in at the last minute and expect immediate hand holding and attention.
- complain about the fee before the return is even finished; or are perpetual fee complainers whenever they receive the bill
- want to know the result or an estimate of the net result before you've been able to complete work on the return.
- do not respond promptly to requests for missing information, and then rush you after they provide it
- demand higher-level personnel work on their return but pay fees commensurate with services of lower-level people.
- want only a partner to call them with questions or will talk only to the top partners.

Some clients we consider as problem clients are those who want extensive hand holding, such as wanting a partner to help them sign the return, make out the tax checks, and take it to the post office for them and have it sent by certified mail (e-filing has reduced mailing returns tremendously), but who don't recognize those services as valuable and worthy of an extra fee. Other problem clients are those who show up unannounced late at night and want to review the papers they previously provided to us with whoever will be working on their return or children of important business clients who expect a same-day or next-day turnaround on their return. Still, other problem clients are those who simply waste our time by showing up for their tax preparation interview unprepared and who sit there opening, discussing, and examining each envelope they received that they think relates to their returns and that they put in a folder to bring to the meeting.

Leveraging Technology 3

Using Software to Its Fullest

Substantial investments are made in technology including the hardware, software, portals, use of the Cloud and security. These are easily measurable costs because they are purchased or contracted for. A measurable loss occurs when there is downtime when software or the systems are not performing. However, unmeasured costs of training and underperforming or underutilization of technology could actually be greater and are sometimes given a short rein in favor of the chargeable hour.

In many firms, and in particular the tax area, training is given in a perfunctory manner. Required times, courses, and demonstrations are scheduled, and then the attendees are sent to do their "regular" work, usually not getting back to what they learned for a while—and certainly not taking time to review what they learned and to practice using the software or systems.

We are trained on two types of new systems: those that require interaction with others, such as logging on to a job, taking responsibility for the next step, and updating our status, and systems that we use to get our job done such as the return's preparation, which is the meat of what we do. Let's look at both of these.

When work tracking software is introduced, it must be followed and used because there is immediate interaction with everyone else who needs to work on that client or matter. An example is when someone who works on a tax return is told that the client's information has come in, has been logged in, has been scanned, and is ready for the preparer to start work on it. The people who will be preparing returns log in and select the return to do based on a first in-first out (FIFO) method. The remaining returns are unassigned, awaiting someone to claim them. Each time a file is opened on the computer, the user is automatically logged in. An administrator checks to make sure returns are selected in order, no files are missed, the time worked is on track with the budget or expectations, and no holes are in the system. People who sleep through the training still learn the system well because they have no choice. The firm management pat themselves on the back for creating effective systems that use technology to its fullest.

Now, let's look at tax research software, data mining software, market data programs, or net meeting applications. Actually, I don't want to lose you and would like your agreement on what I am suggesting, so let's look at the tools and necessities that we can all recognize as being universally used: Word, Outlook, Excel, and Adobe Acrobat. Question: How much training does your firm offer in these four essential programs? Might I suggest that it is very little, if anything at all? Understanding that you have grown-ups working for you, I can recognize that all new versions come with tutorials (none come with instructions anymore—or should I say documentation) and that firm management expects their staff to go through the tutorials because they were told to when the new version was installed. Did you get any training or do the tutorials?

I believe these four basic programs are underutilized and that there is immeasurable time loss due to inefficiencies because of a lack of full understanding of the special features and power of this software. The loss is unmeasured because no one spends blocks of extra time because of their misuse. The loss is not appreciated because everyone uses these programs on a regular, continuous basis and doesn't know what they don't know, and the few who might know, don't want to take the time to learn the programs better because they have a job at hand that needs to be completed.

Looking at what I just wrote, if it were true, it is a sad commentary on us. However, to a great extent, it is true. Because many of these tasks are performed daily, a great time loss occurs without anyone doing something to stop it primarily because they are in very small doses. Here are a few examples.

Word

- Proper use of styles and headings
- Use of "New Window" when you are working on a large document
- Inserting a complete file into a document
- Page numbering of a section of a document

- Clicking to increase and decrease the view size of a document
- Tracking changes
- Inserting ready-made shapes and charts and diagrams
- Pasting special-to-copy formats from one document to another
- Automatic tables of contents
- Inserting footnotes
- Inserting page breaks
- Mail merge
- Addressing envelopes
- Sorting lists
- Formatting tables
- Preparing business plans with templates
- Preparing brochures and flyers
- Changing margins for a footer
- Changing lowercase to all caps or vice versa
- Searching for a key word in a folder
- Spell checking headings
- Eliminating a table but keeping contents in the file
- Removing a hyperlink when entering an e-mail address in the body of a document
- Saving an e-mail into .doc format rather than .txt format
- Scanning your signature and saving it as a .jpg so it can be added into a Word document
- Using "AutoCorrect" for repetitive phrases. Following are some that I use:
  - lm: Let me know that this e-mail was received by replying. Thank you.
  - iaq: If you have any questions, don't hesitate to call me (cell: 1-XXX-XXX-XXXX). Thanks.
  - f/u: follow up
  - s/b: should be
  - iy: If you have any questions or comments, please do not hesitate to call.

Outlook

- Archiving received and sent e-mails
- Assigning classifications to your contacts

- Updating contacts
- Grouping contacts
- Using tasks
- Setting defaults to your appointments
- Managing undone work you assign to yourself
- Keeping a to-do list
- Cleaning up an in-box of accumulated e-mails
- Deactivating an appointment reminder

Excel

- Performing what ifs
- Using preset templates for charts
- Using @If functions and other functions
- Getting rid of the formula correction wizard when a wrong formula is entered
- Applying absolutes in a spreadsheet
- Duplicating formatting
- Transferring data to a Word file
- Including a blank row immediately above the row with a sum to facilitate adding rows and having the sum change to include the added rows

Adobe Acrobat

- Adding notes and printing out a summary of the notes
- Editing a PDF file
- Transferring a PDF to a JPEG file so it can be resized
- Rearranging pages
- Adding and formatting headers and footers on part of a file
- Inserting a signature
- Inserting PDF pages into a Word file
- Converting a PDF file into Word format

I have taken courses in using new software and have been given many tips on its use that I soon forget. The course handbooks become the bible for what I learned. Alternatives, such as buying an instruction book, don't work so well (although I always end up buying such a book—one with lots of pictures) because they are too comprehensive and take too long to show something (and they have poor indexes).

Two solutions to underutilizations are short, 20-minute, 1-on-1 walkthroughs or a 1-hour course with a handout that covers the course. The basic use of the software, along with tips and shortcuts, would be covered. This training would be supplemented by a go-to person who is thoroughly familiar with the software and who could address any questions. This go-to person could be from the IT or administrative department or an accountant more experienced with that software. The point is that the questions should be made easy to be answered. Doing so has a cost but a much greater benefit or dividend because of more effective use of the software.

I've just discussed standard software everyone uses. Now let's cover tax preparation software. Careful and deliberate training should now be given to tax preparation software and should include training from people more familiar with pieces of it, such as transferring data to multiple states or rollovers of items from prior years' returns.

During tax season, it is particularly important to have someone who preparers can turn to. Not getting effective assistance quickly can result in the preparer spending extra time or making repetitive errors on multiple returns before he or she get to a reviewer who can spot the error. But no one can watch the wasted or incorrect efforts or steps put into the return. I suggest that the designated experts for the tax preparation software walk around and observe preparers, on a spot basis, watching their work and offering assistance. I have seen this done, and given the high concentration of tax preparation during tax season, especially during nights and weekend days that are dedicated to business or individual tax preparation, I have seen great results. Training is not a cost but an investment, and it's a high dividend paying investment during any period of intense repetitive work. I have seen this work and highly endorse this method.

Many software training programs are generic and really do not address the specific issues many users actually have. For that reason, I recommend short training sessions with user-specific pointers and a go-to person thoroughly familiar with the software.

Peer-to-Peer

I have gotten into the habit of calling people over to watch me do something on a file (when I am about to do it) that I think is not being done by that person. Sometimes, when I show someone something, they reciprocate by showing me one of their shortcuts or power uses. So now we both gain with our informal show and tell. Peer-to-peer training is highly effective. Your firm culture should encourage and support this.

Update Handbooks, Forms, Services, and Software

At my firm, every staff person is given his or her own copies of one volume tax guides for the IRS. Others who request them are also given the tax guides for individual states they work on. Many staff, including myself, have gotten very proficient in searching the web to obtain answers they need. Many times the search leads to the IRS or state tax agency instruction booklets. I think these are underutilized resources. A suggestion to increase proficiency and familiarly with the tax guides is to have staff people complete the CPE quiz for the tax guides. This also provides low-cost CPE credit. All staff needing any additional materials or anything extra for their homes are given it.

The one-volume tax guides I refer to are the CCH *U.S. Master Tax Guide*, the *RIA Federal Tax Handbook*, and *J.K. Lasser's Your Income Tax—Professional Edition*. Lasser also has a regular edition—also wonderful—that is sold in every bookstore in the country. The difference is that the professional edition has citations and references.

We have an extensive and complete tax library, all on the Internet, with no paper books or physical library except for the one-volume tax guides provided to staff, but they are also available in digital versions for those that prefer it. We also have licenses for the people who will use selected services.

The tax department, besides being the tax planning, research, and review arm of the firm, is a resource and support center for the staff. However, before any work is referred to the tax department, it should be first checked in the one-volume tax guide or the applicable instruction form. All referred questions should be presented in writing by e-mail, with a copy to the engagement partner. The e-mail forces the person requesting the research to work out and clearly articulate what he or she needs. This requirement keeps the researcher focused. I have also found that the person laying out the issue in writing can many times uncover his or her own answer or realize that there is no need to continue with that question or line of approach. The research request also needs to include a budgeted time and a client to be charged. A researcher needs to value his or her own time and this written request will stop unnecessary or wasted efforts on behalf of someone who hasn't thought things through.

Members of the AICPA Tax Section have access to extensive checklists, which are excellent tools to use when preparing and reviewing returns. The preparers can use the checklists not only to do a better job of making sure they did not miss anything but as a self-review before handing in the return to the reviewer. Many of the checklists come in a short version as well as a full version. The 1040 checklist comes in 3 versions: a 2-page mini checklist, a 9-page short checklist, and a 28-page full checklist.

Many firms keep the last dozen years' *U.S. Master Tax Guides* and IRS federal and state Package Xs in their libraries. These have tax rates and depreciation schedules and rates as well as the tax rules for those years. They can be very helpful if you need to prepare prior year returns for clients who have not filed timely. Again, we are throwing away paper versions as the information becomes available online. We have access to most everything online and no longer clutter our offices with the books.

Keeping current is not only a tax season issue but also an important part of your professional activity. You should scan business and professional journals, periodicals, and newsletters the moment they come to you—either in print or digital versions. Spend a few minutes seeing what issues and topics are covered. If any issues relate to a client, either look at this information more carefully or put it in the client's file (paper or electronic—I will no longer distinguish between type of files—I will just refer to files). Then schedule time to work on the issues. This whole process should not take more than 2–3 minutes per publication. If you receive 5–10 such newsletters and e-mails per week, then 30 minutes per week is the most time that you'll spend to "get smarter" and be able to serve clients the best way possible.

Research Materials—Finding a Quick Answer

Here are some of the first places to look for a quick answer. Note that I use the following guides alternatively. If you use more than one guide, you can do the following exercise with the books you use. If you only use one guidebook, perhaps you should consider adding a second one.

- CCH's *U.S. Master Tax Guide*
- *RIA Federal Tax Handbook*
- *J.K. Lasser's Your Income Tax—Professional Edition*
- *Tax agency instruction books*
- Looking it up online

I use all five of these resources, depending on the issue. FYI, I do a lot of writing and blogging and answer scores of writer and client questions each year. I really need to be able to get quick answers. I also used all of these resources for some of the same questions, so I have developed a preference for one of these resources over the other. To apply guidance to my staff and colleagues, I developed a rating system to show which source is the best place to go for most quick answers, as follows:

Answers found in less than:	EM* Rating
5 minutes	10
5–10 minutes	5
Over 10 minutes	0

* I recommend that you use this system to develop your own first choice resource and then use it more than the others.

		EM Rating				
No.	**Question**	**CCH**	**RIA**	**JKL**	**Instr.**	**Online**
1	Q: Are day care costs paid by an employer to a third party organization income to the employee or excludible? A:					
2	Q: A client over age 59½ rolled over his or her IRA into a Roth IRA on December 20, 2012. When is the earliest he or she can withdraw it and not be subject to tax or penalty? A:					
3	Q: What is the taxable income when a client settles her credit card debt of $80,000 using $20,000 that her employer loaned to her? Immediately after settling the credit card debt, the client also owed $8,000 to her employer for a prior loan. She had no other debt or assets. A:					
4	Q: Can someone over age 50 who is covered by his or her employer's 401(k) plan and maximizes his or her catch-up amount also contribute the maximum catch-up to a nondeductible IRA? A:					
5	Q: What is the minimum amount of self-employment income (assuming no other earned income is reported) that will qualify for four quarters of Social Security coverage for 20XX? A:					
6	Q: Does an employee who receives employer securities as part of a distribution from his or her 401(k) plan and does not roll it over to an IRA but has it taxed have to pay the 10 percent excise tax if he or she is under age 59½? A:					

(continued)

		EM Rating				
No.	**Question**	**CCH**	**RIA**	**JKL**	**Instr.**	**Online**
7	Q: What is the tax and penalty if the person who set up a Section 529 plan in 2011 with $12,000 for his or her 6-year-old grandchild closes the account in 2015 and takes back the $9,000 that is left in the account? A:					
8	Q: Does a father who gives his daughter $19,000 to pay off her college loans (which was used for her tuition) need to file a gift tax return and pay any gift tax? A:					
9	Q: How are $30,000 short term capital losses carried over from one year offset against the next year's $20,000 short term gains and $20,000 long term gains? A:					
10	Q: Can losses sustained because of an alleged Bernard Madoff-type of fraud be deductible in full as a casualty loss and not be limited by 10 percent of adjusted gross income, plus $100? A:					
	Total rating					

Which resource do you turn to first for a quick answer?

The person reviewing your tax returns should be more adept at finding these answers than a preparer. Also, how adept are non-tax specialist partners that think they "know" taxes? Consider giving your reviewers a test (see chapter 13).

Every one of these questions was looked up by me in more than one source—some in all five sources. I had trouble finding the answers to each question and became very annoyed when it took excessive time and effort to get the answer.

During the time that I was writing this book, I was the "tax expert" on an online chat for an hour and wanted to have some tax resources I could refer to when I gave my responses. I used a one volume tax handbook, various IRS instruction books and the individual tax forms in front of me. . I was lucky. I either knew the answer to every question or was able to find it quickly. Many of the questions were answered by looking at the actual forms.

Websites to Search

You can use many websites to get quick tax answers and get pointed in the right direction for major questions you need answered. Searching the Internet is a lot easier than getting up and thumbing through a book for answers.

Following are some helpful tax websites that I use. I would appreciate any feedback on websites you regularly visit for your tax questions.

- www.irs.gov—An excellent website that is searchable and can put any IRS form and instructions in front of you in approximately 30 seconds.
- www.ustaxcourt.gov—The United States Tax Court's website includes all cases from May 1986 to present and is searchable.
- www.pwacpa.com—This is Barry Picker's website, which has a useful range of tax article links. Go here to find quick answers to many of your questions or to get ideas of discussions you can have with clients.
- www.fidelity.com or www.schwab.com or many other major brokerage firms—They have excellent websites, with a wide variety of resources covered and explained.
- www.360financialliteracy.org—This AICPA-maintained website features a tremendous range of financial and tax information aimed at lay people. The website also covers planning for every life stage. There are charts you can print and use with clients.
- www.feedthepig.org—This AICPA-maintained website helps Americans aged 25 to 34 spend and save more thoughtfully. It includes several interactive tools.
- www.google.com/finance—This website permits you to search the historic cost of stocks. After working through the website's navigation a couple of times, you'll be able to get what you need in less than 30 seconds. (P.S. I hope you charge the client extra for this "service." He or she was either too lazy to look it up or figured it was easier if you did it, without placing any value on your time.)

- www.moneymattersnj.com—This website is run by the New Jersey Society of Certified Public Accountants and has searchable articles.
- www.withum.com—My firm's website has some great articles and tax tips. In addition, most large CPA and law firm websites have searchable articles.
- www.leimberg.com—This website has links to many websites and is organized by topic, making it a good first stop as you research. Leimberg also has an e-newsletter that I subscribe to for updates on estate, gift, retirement and financial planning. There is a charge, but if you are seriously involved in those areas, it is well worth the money.
- www.yahoo.com—Many times, I just type in the topic or issue I am working on and let Yahoo search and give me suggestions of where the answers may be.
- www.natptax.com—The National Association of Tax Professionals (NATP) website is also a great first stop, with a wide offering of links to specific subject sites. I am a member of the NATP, and I get frequent e-newsletters that are well worth the annual membership fee. The NATP also offers members a tax research service at very nominal fees (with a yearly freebie) for most questions.

Complete Pre-Year-End Planning for Select Clients 4

Pre-year-end planning for clients starts in late October and continues through December. We try to make the meeting last no longer than one hour. Several approaches exist to the pre-year-end planning meeting. This chapter describes a few ways of handling it and adds a word about identifying cross-sell opportunities.

Tax Projections Review

Different types of tax season clients exist. Projections would typically be prepared for those with higher incomes, uncertain and varying income, or unusual transactions during the year, as well as those who are subject to the alternative minimum tax or whose returns are affected by year-end actions.

Many clients obviously need projections; others are not as clearly in need, so it is important to alert clients when to contact you for a projection. We also prepare projections for most of the new clients we get toward the end of the year.

Preparing projections serves as a tool to guide clients into what they can do to reduce their taxes by speeding up deductions or deferring income, or sometimes vice versa if they are subject to the Alternative Minimum Tax. Projections also provide an opportunity to review a client's financial situation and allow concentrated, unrushed time to discuss a client's tax or overall financial affairs (or both). Furthermore, projections provide a road map that a reviewer can use to compare with the actual return to make sure there are no overlooked items.

Projections are typically prepared twice per year for most clients: once when the tax return is prepared and a second time toward the end of the year when most of the results are known. For clients with changing or widely varying income, projections could be prepared before each estimated tax due date. This is not necessary for clients with increasing income because you would use the previous year's tax as the basis for the estimated tax. However, for clients with very large but dropping income, you might want to calculate the lowest necessary payment. When the return is worked on, the interviewer will ask the client questions about the expected current year's income or changes from the previous year. This information is needed to prepare the estimated tax returns and serves as a guide to the client's current year situation. The interviewer is usually a higher-level staff person or partner. If the information is sent in without an interview, the preparer (usually a lower-level staff member) will call the client to collect the information needed for the projection, but it then should be reviewed by a partner.

At the end of the year, a partner or manager-level staff person should meet with the client to discuss the situation for the year and the expected outcome, as well as the opportunities for year-end tax planning.

In some cases, the projection could be done only during the preparation of the tax return and then followed up with a phone call to the client toward the end of the year to determine if there are any major changes and to discuss the year-end tax planning.

I enjoy the pre-year-end meetings with clients. It gives me an opportunity to discuss his or her affairs, concerns, and what's on his or her mind to see what true planning can be done.

When there is no meeting, and the information is obtained otherwise, someone from the firm will send the client a copy of the worksheet and will arrange to discuss it over the phone. In situations when there are major changes that result in large amounts of taxes that will be due, the partner most knowledgeable about the client will call and discuss it.

By the time we are done, we have reviewed the projections numerous times with many of our clients—with some clients it is done almost monthly.

Projections take time and have a cost. In some instances, clients are billed specifically for the projection. Clients on a strict time billing basis will get charged for all the time in that process. Clients on an annual fixed fee for their tax preparation and other services will not be billed and the projection will be part of the service. Another method is for clients on fixed fees to get a shopping list of services with prices for each of them and the services which include projections are like a sunk cost because many times there is no separate review of the fee structure.

There are a few pricing issues here. I question what a client on a time billing basis would say if he or she knew the cost of the projection and how the CPA would justify the value. Secondly, many accountants with clients on a fixed fee might have started out with projections and now do them as a rote service without questioning the need for it or value to the client, yet the accountants have the cost. Third, clients' situations continually change, thus also changing the need and use for the projections; especially when the client's situation has stabilized for a number of years. In many instances, the projection done when the tax return is worked on followed up by a pre-year-end phone call is the lowest cost method and can capture any major changes that will affect the tax payments. A secondary use of the projection is to use the worksheet to report any changes or expected changes and when the return is worked on, this will serve as a notice to make sure this information is provided by the client.

Exhibit 4-1, "Sample Tax Projection Memo," is a sample memo accompanying a tax projection we sent to a client. This memo helps make the projection and information we give the client user-friendly and reduces the need or urgency for a face-to-face meeting. A discussion over the telephone or via e-mail can do it.

EXHIBIT 4-1 Sample Tax Projection Memo

To: [*Client Name*]
From: [*Partner Name*]
Date: November 15, 20XX
Re: Year-end planning

Enclosed is your updated 20XX and 20YY tax projection. Included is a summary of your last three years' tax returns.

To prepare the projection, we made certain estimates as follows:

Wages	Projected from pay stub
Interest, dividends, and capital gain distributions	Used same amounts as last year
Capital gains (sale of your employer's stock)	1/3/XX sold 10,000 shares ($250,000 less cost of $20,000) Estimated capital gain: $230,000 7/3/XX sold 20,000 shares ($550,000 less cost $40,000) Estimated capital gain: $510,000 Please verify the proceeds and costs on both transactions.
Pension excess contributions	Same as last year
Partnership income from family real estate partnerships	Combined income of $55,000

New S corporation investment	Assumed no profit or loss
Itemized deductions	Estimates based on last year and current year information that we have
Exercise of incentive stock options	You exercised options for 50,000 shares at $5 per share; the stock's value at date of exercise was $25. Tax preference income for AMT purposes was estimated at $1,000,000.

- Your projected 20XX federal tax is $666,666. The New York State and City tax is projected at $222,222.
- Your payments to date are listed on the attached projection sheet. Please verify that you made them.
- The balance due, which should be paid between January 1 and January 15, 20XX, is as follows:
  — IRS $ 90,000
  — State of New York $ 40,000

* *Note that the NYS tax should be paid in January because of the AMT you are subject to for 20XX. Paying the tax in 20XX would give you ZERO federal tax benefit.*

- We would like an updated stock option plan schedule.
- Please send us a copy of the closing statement for the purchase of your vacation home.
- Please be aware that you might be able to use stock you presently own at the full FMV to pay for the stock you acquire by exercising your options.

If you have any questions or comments after reviewing the enclosed projection, or if you do not agree with some of the estimates, please do not hesitate to call.

Line-by-Line Review

We developed a new service: meeting clients in the summer and reviewing their return with them, line by line. This accomplishes a number of things. It is done at a less hectic time; creates an opportunity to involve the clients on a more proactive basis on their tax return; is a good way to discuss financial planning, as well as tax planning, with the clients; and opens up a time for the clients to share their life goals.

Occasionally, we find errors on the tax return, although that is not the purpose of this meeting. We then have to make a determination with the client whether an amended return is to be prepared and filed. In some cases, we tell the client that the amended return will be done when we prepare the client's return the following year.

Unprotected Estimates Review

In the case of tax returns in which we do not "protect" the client with the estimated tax payments, we put the estimated tax payment due dates on our tax control so we can follow up during the year before the June, September, and final estimated tax payment deadline.

We also put the estimated tax payments on our tax control for selected clients based on their needs and our involvement with them. In those cases, we would send the client the estimated tax forms approximately two weeks before the due date. A sample notice is included as exhibit 4-2, "Sample Unprotected Estimated Tax Payment Notice."

Any unprotected client is a candidate for a projection. We ask such clients to call us approximately two weeks before the estimated payment due date if there are any changes in their situation. During that call, we define a change. A *change* is an increase or decrease of more than 25 percent in their regular income stream; a sale of an asset not typically expected to be sold, such as a business; a change in their marital status; a purchase or the formation of a business; an inheritance or expected inheritance; an unexpected disaster; winning the lottery; commencing or ending a lawsuit for financial damages; receiving or exercising stock options or employer securities; or getting a large promotion or the separation or retirement from their job. Additionally, we will call many of these clients without waiting for them to call us.

EXHIBIT 4-2 Sample Unprotected Estimated Tax Payment Notice

IMPORTANT NOTICE

To:	[*Client Name*]
From:	[*Partner Name*]
Date:	[Date]
Re:	Unprotected estimated tax payments

Please note that the combination of your projected withholding and/or estimated tax payments for 20XX is not the required amount to "protect" you from the penalty for underpayment of estimated taxes.

We based the estimated payments on information you provided to us about your expected 20XX tax situation. If you believe these amounts are not accurate, or you want to be fully protected, please call us immediately.

We further suggest that you call us to review your situation before each estimated tax payment is due, as follows:

Payment due date	**Call us by**
June 15	June 1
September 15	September 1
January 15, 20YY	December 15

If you have any questions or comments, please do not hesitate to call.

Cross-Sell Opportunities

Almost every tax client needs additional services we can provide. The issue becomes not how to approach them with the suggestions but when. Not doing so takes away an opportunity to better serve the client and for you to improve your revenue and client relationship. We collect copies of the tax return summaries, Excel spreadsheets or pages 1 and 2 of the returns. The summaries are reviewed by a partner to determine if there are additional tax or financial planning opportunities with which to help the client. We also specifically review all clients with a Schedule C to see if a pension plan is applicable, and if so, we call them. We suggest opening a Keogh plan; 401(k) plan, simplified employee pension (SEP) plan; SIMPLE IRA; defined benefit plans; nonstatutory option plans; and deferred compensation plans, when appropriate.

We have compiled a listing of clients' birth dates and make notes about which clients might have to take required minimum distributions from IRAs and, if the client has multiple accounts, from which account to take the withdrawal. Calls or alerts to these clients a year in advance is a goodwill gesture and allows for planning to determine if there could be a benefit to the client.

We also prepare follow-up lists when we review the tax returns for additional services we can perform for the clients after tax season ends. We start calling clients around the middle of June. Note that if the additional service is time sensitive, it should not be delayed; a partner should be advised and should make arrangements to help the client in a timely and appropriate manner.

Exhibit 4-3, "Sample Checklist of Follow-up Items," is a sample of the types of items that can be followed up on. This exhibit was taken from an actual follow-up list prepared during tax season as returns were worked on.

EXHIBIT 4-3 Sample Checklist of Follow-up Items

________: Trust situs of trustee. Consider changing re: NYS tax.

________: Payroll taxes.

________: Household employee payroll taxes.

________: Provide our Journal Entries to client for them to put on their books

________: Letter re: using a complete set of books with B/S as well as P&L for client's Schedule C

________: Review partner's cash distributions and percents on the K-1. The 20XX distributions do not seem right.

________: To review loan & exchange account. There seems to be too many old items

________: Review investment income.

________: Review potential retirement income.

________:

Review IRA and pension designations and compare to what client says they want accomplished

IRA and pension designations should be coordinated with clients' estate planning

________: Suggest to client that because she has real estate taxable income, if she were to invest in additional real estate properties, the initial losses could shelter the real estate income she has. Maybe that could enable her to be more aggressive.

________: Follow up and tell the client how to specifically identify stocks and mutual fund shares to be sold, or that can be donated to charities rather than the cash payments they are presently making

Day traders: Does Mark to Market apply to their non-proprietary transactions?

________: Recommend that the client consolidate personal retirement accounts, perhaps into one IRA rollover account. Need to obtain details and distribution choices from present trustees.

________: Client's negative capital account will be "taxable" at a later time. Ask client if he or she wants us to suggest planning alternatives.

________, ________, ________: Meet with client in June or July for line-by-line tax return review and planning session.

________: Call after September to follow up doing year-end tax planning

________: Call client ASAP to consider additional withholding tax now.

________: Explain cashless exercise of ISO to avoid AMT.

________: Follow up to perform Financial Planning: meet by end of April. Combine and invest various retirement accounts and coordinate an asset allocation plan.

________: Stock options; look at it.

________: Get info on client's employer or company from Web (if possible).

________: Suggest that client should consider setting up an organized charity for his activities—501(c)(3) vs. foundation, or donor advised fund

________: Prepare amended return to correct K-1 allocations.

________: Client is required to file a delinquent Form 5500 for last two years

________: Tell client how to set up SIMPLE plan for this year.

________: Discuss what client is doing with the "scholarship" from business for daughter's tuition.

________: Check out anticipated cash distributions from inherited IRA.

________: Calculate tax for H and W separately.

________: Financial planning re: retirement income.

________: Suggest a family limited partnership to consolidate family investing and control.

________: Effects of wash sale and doubling up now and selling original shares in 31 days.

Complete Mailings to Clients 5

You'll make several mailings to clients in the course of a year: a pre-year-end newsletter to be mailed in November, tax organizers to be mailed in mid-January, a possible letter regarding a tax notice service and maybe a privacy notification. This chapter discusses each of these types of mailings.

Mailings

A word about mailings. There are two types of mailings: postal and email. These are now used interchangeably—do whatever you think works best for you. There are appropriate times for both. I personally like to postal mail things, especially newsletters and organizers. Emails can be used for updates or one-topic newsletters and can be sent out quicker and more frequently. The reason I like to mail newsletters is that they usually sit on the clients' desks for a while and they can easily be passed on to someone else—emails can be forwarded but most emails are not opened. The purpose of the newsletter is to provide information, show an expertise, keep in touch, show availability and put something tangible in the clients' hands.

Mailing organizers is a promotional tool because it indicates a database of prior information, creating the impression that we are "too important" to drop since we have the client's history which might not be so easily transferred. We send the organizer to everyone except those who ask us not to.

Portals are more secure and many firms are providing passwords for clients to access their information this way.

From here on forward, the use of the word mailing will cover any method you can use to provide information to clients.

Pre-Year-End Newsletter

A pre-year-end newsletter is sent out for both informational and promotional purposes.

By corresponding with our clients during the year and trying to get them to come in for a pre-year-end review, we maintain some semblance of a year-round service. Doing this solidifies the relationship and also makes the person think of us as his or her firm, rather than thinking of any one individual as his or her accountant and not just a tax-preparation service. We also try to encourage clients when we prepare their return to call us during the year if there are changes in their lifestyle, such as a divorce, a new job, a retirement, or an inheritance. And we try to continuously mention trigger events in our newsletters and other correspondence, so clients will know to call us when their taxes might be affected.

Following is a sample 2013 year-end tax planning letter sent to clients. The dates have been kept since some of the information is likely to change. The letter has been included so you can see a sample of an actual letter and not something that is in newsletter format. Also this letter was postal mailed to each client.

2013 Year-End Tax Planning

November 4, 2013

Dear Client:

Our tax system for the most part remains firmly based upon the calendar year. At year-end, a snapshot of your income, deductions, and credits is taken. Based on that data, your tax liability for the year is computed. Year-end tax strategies implemented before your tax liability is "set in stone" can therefore make a significant difference in what you owe for the 2013 tax year, which is now drawing to a close.

Tax planning for year-end 2013 should use both traditional year-end strategies as well as those that react to situations unique to this year. Particularly important at year-end 2013 is the impact of certain tax benefits scheduled to end with 2013; a look ahead at possible sea-changes in the tax laws starting in 2015; and attention to new opportunities and pitfalls created during the past year through court cases and IRS rulings.

Income and Deduction Shifting

The traditional year-end strategy of income shifting applies to year-end 2013 but with an extra twist. Under traditional strategy, you time your income and deductions so that your taxable income is about even for 2013 and 2014 so your tax bracket does not spike in either 2013 or 2014. If you anticipate a higher tax bracket for 2014, you may want to accelerate income into 2013 and defer deductions into 2014. If you anticipate a leaner 2014, income might be delayed through deferred compensation arrangements, postponing year-end bonuses, maximizing deductible retirement contributions, and delaying year-end billings.

The twist for year-end 2012 is the uncertain future for tax rates after 2013. Many political observers forecast that higher-income taxpayers will be asked to pay more, either through higher tax rates or more limited deductions. That may suggest a strategy in which income is not deferred but is recognized now at lower tax rates still available in 2012 and 2013. Our office will keep you posted on developments.

Roth Conversions

If you converted an individual retirement account (IRA) to a Roth IRA in 2010, you were given an option: recognize all income in 2010 or defer that income, half into 2011 and half into 2012. If you elected to defer that income into 2011 and 2012, do not forget to figure that income into your year-end planning for 2011.

If you initiated a Roth conversion earlier in 2011 and that Roth account has declined in value since then, you should consider a "Roth reconversion." Reconverting your Roth IRA back to a regular IRA before year-end will allow you to avoid paying income tax on an account balance at its higher value.

Finally, if you have not yet made a Roth conversion, doing so at year-end 2011 might be an opportunity worth serious consideration. Variables include your present income tax bracket, how close you are to retirement, and your access to other funds both to pay the conversion tax and to delay distributions from your Roth account later. Our office can help you make the right decision.

AMT

Because the AMT was not indexed for inflation, and for other reasons, the AMT today encroaches on many moderate-income taxpayers, especially two-income married couples. With most of your income and deductions for 2012 more predictable as year-end approaches, now is a good time to compute whether you will be subject to the AMT for 2012 or 2013. Our office can explore whether certain deductions should be more evenly divided between 2012 and 2013 and which deductions will qualify, or will not be as valuable, for AMT purposes.

Capital Gains and Losses

Our office can also help you time the recognition of capital gains and losses at year-end to minimize your net capital gains tax and maximize deductible capital losses. Many investors have excess capital losses from recent stock market declines that they may now "carry over" to offset capital gains that would otherwise be taxable.

Also of concern is whether the maximum tax rate for capital gains will rise from 15 percent to 20 percent or higher after year-end 2012 because of the scheduled expiration of the Bush-era tax cuts. Because long-term capital gains are only available on stocks and other capital assets held for more than one year, a capital asset must be bought on or before December 30, 2012, in order to be sold in 2013 and guarantee qualifying under the lower capital gains rates. We can help you coordinate your year-end trades with these tax variables in mind.

Finally, if you would like capital gains taxes at a zero percent rate, consider investing in "Section 1202" small business stock before year end. The 2010 Tax Relief Act allows the exclusion of 100 percent of the gain from the sale or exchange of qualified small business stock acquired by an individual after September 27, 2010, and before January 1, 2012, and held for more than five years. The window of opportunity to invest in stock that will yield 100 percent tax-free gain closes on December 31, 2011.

Payroll Taxes

All wage earners and self-employed individuals will experience a tax increase in 2012 unless Congress extends the current employee-side payroll tax cut. For calendar year 2011, the employee-share of OASDI taxes is reduced from 6.2 percent to 4.2 percent up the Social Security wage base of $106,800 (self-employed individuals receive a comparable benefit). President Obama has proposed to extend and enhance the payroll tax cut. The fate of the payroll tax cut will likely be decided by Congress late in 2011.

Life Changes

Marriage, divorce, the birth of a child, death, a change in job or loss of a job, and retirement are just some of the life events that trigger a special urgency for year-end tax planning. If you have had a life change, please contact our office so we can review how that change will impact your federal tax liability. After December 31, 2013, it will be too late to alter most of your bottom-line tax liability for 2013.

Medical Expenses

Effective January 1, 2011, the *Patient Protection and Affordable Care Act (PPACA)* provides that over-the-counter medications and drugs can no longer be reimbursed from a health flexible spending arrangement (health FSA) unless a prescription is obtained. The rule also applies to health reimbursement arrangements (HRAs), health savings accounts (HSAs), and Archer medical savings accounts (Archer MSAs), an important consideration for employees who are required to make a decision by year-end 2012 on how much to fund their accounts in 2013.

Tax Extenders

A number of tax extenders are scheduled to expire after December 31, 2011. They include the following items:

- the state and local sales tax deduction;
- the higher education tuition deduction; and
- the teacher's classroom expense deduction.

Seniors age 70½ and older should also consider making a charitable contribution directly from their IRAs up to $100,000 and paying no tax on the distribution. This tax break, especially advantageous to those who do not itemize deductions, is scheduled to end for distributions made in tax years beginning after December 31, 2011.

Casualty Losses

Taxpayers in many states experienced natural disasters in 2012. A casualty loss can result from the damage, destruction or loss to your property from any sudden, unexpected or unusual event—such as a hurricane, earthquake, wildfire, or flood. Casualty losses are generally deductible in the year the casualty occurred, less 10 percent of your adjusted gross income and a $100 per-casualty deductible.

However, if you have a casualty loss from a federally declared disaster, you can elect to treat the loss as having occurred in the year immediately preceding the tax year in which the disaster happened, and you can deduct the loss on your return or amended return for that preceding tax year. The election gives taxpayers the opportunity to maximize their tax savings in the year in which the savings will be greatest.

Energy Tax Incentives

If you are considering replacing your roof, HVAC system, or windows and doors, doing so using energy-efficient materials before January 1, 2013, may generate tax savings. Through the end of 2012, a number of residential energy-efficiency improvements qualify for a tax credit. These include qualified windows and doors, insulation products, HVAC systems, and roofing. The "lifetime" credit amount for 2012, however, is $500 and no more than $200 of the credit amount can be attributed to exterior windows and skylights. Please call our office for details.

Gift and Estate Tax

The current estate tax through 2013 is set at a maximum 35 percent rate and a $5 million exemption amount. Many experts predict that after 2013, Congress will lower the exclusion to $3.5 million and raise the top rate to 45 percent. In light of this possibility, lifetime gift-giving, ideally on an annual basis, should continue to form part of a master estate plan. The annual gift tax exclusion per donee on which no gift tax is due is $13,000 for 2012 (and, again, for 2013), with $26,000 allowed to each donee by married couples. Making a gift at year-end 2011 to take advantage of this annual, per-donee exclusion should be considered by anyone with even modest wealth.

If you have any questions about the tax provisions and year-end planning techniques described in this letter, please contact our office.

Sincerely yours,

Jane Smith, CPA
John Doe, CPA

Smith and Doe CPAs LLP

Tax Organizers

Two sample cover letters for mailing organizers are included as exhibit 5-1, "Sample Organizer Cover Letter—Short Version," and exhibit 5-2, "Sample Organizer Cover Letter—Long Version."

The only clients who do not get the organizers are those who specifically request that they not be sent. We also make sure that they are not sent to clients' spouses' homes when they are separated or to minor children or children at college (especially when large trust funds are in their name and their parents or grandparents have not told them about it) or under any other special circumstances. We make sure that the organizers are not sent to prior addresses.

Included in the letter is a sentence or two that explains extra billing situations. We now bill extra for work that is not a tax preparation process, such as calculating a stock's basis, helping a client determine the basis of an asset that is sold especially a vacation home or rental property, reviewing a divorce or separation agreement and determining taxable alimony, and calculating a net operating loss deduction. The extra billing is identified as such and is included with the tax preparation fee.

You can try getting additional tax return business by sending a blank organizer with a cover letter asking your client to give the extra organizer to anyone he or she knows that the client thinks might need your services. It is not costly and one or two new clients can make it profitable. An additional benefit is that this lets your clients know you are looking to grow or for additional business and to plant this in their minds and eventually could lead them to refer you to a business client or special assignments.

Clients are starting to request electronic organizers. We e-mail the organizer to clients, and they enter their information and e-mail it back to us or print the organizer and complete it. We now ask clients how they want their organizers sent postal.

We also sent an e-file procedure information sheet with the organizers. An example is included in exhibit 5-3, "Sample E-file Procedures Information Sheet."

Many firms send engagement letters with the organizers, some send rate schedules, and some send pre-bills. I haven't found any overwhelmingly great method, and each firm seems to do what it feels comfortable with and what works for them.

Some firms do not send organizers, but they send a checklist of what should be sent to them. (See exhibit 5-4, "Information Checklist Sent to Clients.") The firms feel that the filling out of the organizer creates more work for them because they have to reconcile the client's errors. Also, they prefer to work off the original documents and actual back-up documents of the client or the memos and notes the client sends to them.

EXHIBIT 5-1 Sample Organizer Cover Letter—Short Version

20XX

Please be sure to read the important information below!

January 20XX

To Our Clients:

Enclosed you will find your 20WW personal income tax organizer. Please complete as much of the organizer and the enclosed addendum sheet as possible and return it to our office at your earliest convenience.

Once you have received substantially all of your tax information, please send it to us with the enclosed organizer so that we can begin the preparation process. The sooner that you supply us with your information, the sooner we will be able to prepare your tax returns in a timely and efficient manner, avoiding the possibility of having to obtain an extension of time to file.

The IRS and most government tax agencies prefer and request that taxpayers e-file their tax returns. Unless you tell us otherwise, or circumstances do not permit, your federal and state returns will be e-filed. E-filing will permit you to receive your refunds much faster than filing the returns by regular mail. Please note that on e-filed returns, refunds do not have to be directly deposited into your bank account, and any balance due can be paid by check or submitted electronically by the due date of the return, even if the return has been e-filed on an earlier date.

If you wish your tax refunds to be credited directly to your bank account, please review the organizer to make sure that your current banking information is entered and correct.

In prior years, paper copies of tax returns were supplied to you for your records. We now supply copies of your tax returns in PDF format on a CD or through access on our secure client portal. If you regularly use our portal, that is the method that will be used this year; otherwise, the CD format will be used for your copies. If you want paper copies of your returns, please request it when you provide your tax information.

Because certain tax calculations are based on age, please review and enter in the organizer your date of birth, including the dates of birth for your spouse and children.

Please take care in the preparation of your organizer. When possible, supply us with either the original or copies of your tax documents (including "proof" of how your federal and state estimated taxes were paid) so that we may determine the proper tax consequences of each item or transaction.

Protective estimates can be utilized to avoid underestimation penalties. You can avoid a penalty by paying 100 percent (110 percent if your 20XX adjusted gross income was in excess of $150,000) of your 20XX tax as an estimate toward your 20YY tax liability.

Take extra care in completing the section of the organizer regarding your 20YY estimated tax. The proper estimation of your tax will prevent the assessment of penalties. Unless you indicate otherwise, a protective estimate will be prepared for 20YY.

Be sure to indicate or update your telephone numbers and e-mail addresses on the "Taxpayer Information" page of the organizer. Doing so will enable us to quickly resolve any open items associated with the completion of your tax returns.

Please note the rules regarding the substantiation of charitable contributions. The deduction for clothing and household items is prohibited, unless such goods are in good used condition or better. The charitable deduction for automobiles has more stringent rules that must be adhered to in order to claim a tax deduction. In addition, any contribution over $250 must be acknowledged by the charity in a letter, and cash contributions, regardless of the amount, must be supported by a cancelled check, bank record, or receipt from the donee organization showing the name of the organization and the date and amount of the contribution.

Your federal and state tax returns will be prepared from the information you furnish to us. We will not audit or verify the data you submit, although we may ask you for clarification of some of the information.

Release of Your Tax Information to Third Parties

Regulations released under the Internal Revenue Code require tax return preparers to obtain a specific release from their clients in order to supply tax information or copies of tax returns to third parties. Please be aware that if you request copies of your tax returns to be sent to banks or other third parties, we cannot comply with your request until you send us your specific signed authorization. We can, however, send the requested copy of your tax return directly to you for forwarding on to third parties. Please note that the signed authorization must be in a specific format (which we can provide to you) and that we must receive it before your tax return is completed and sent to you for your signature.

Please return the completed organizer and any additional information in the envelope provided. This will enable us to expedite the preparation of your returns.

If you have any questions regarding the preceding, or need help in completing any portion of the organizer, please do not hesitate to contact us.

Very truly yours,

WithumSmith+Brown, P.C.

This letter was prepared by Ronald L. Bleich and is used through the courtesy of WithumSmith+Brown, New Brunswick, NJ.

Letter Sent With Organizer from Abo and Company, LLC

Dear Client,

We are pleased to have the opportunity to assist you in your 20XX tax return preparation and 20YY tax planning. In order to expedite your handling and our mutual processing of the enclosed documents, we have prepared this short list as an overview of what needs to be accomplished:

1. Enclosed is your 20XX tax return organizer for use in compiling the information needed to efficiently process your tax returns. It is our experience that some clients use this organizer consistently and find it quite helpful in organizing their data, but others have developed a process for gathering the pertinent information that works for them and is organized well enough for us to follow and comprehend. We would encourage you to use the organizer to the extent you can because we find this tool to be most helpful in the required process. For continuing clients, 20WW tax return figures are included for the appropriate categories for reference as you input 20XX data. Items such as Form W-2, Form 1099, and Schedule K-1 can simply be attached to the respective pages so that we can input and verify the required figures directly from the source forms. If you need additional space or have questions as you compile information, use the blank spaces provided. This will assure both of us that no information has been overlooked and will help contain fees. Call if you have questions on using the organizer.
2. If this is the first year we are preparing your returns and you haven't done so already, you should provide us copies of last year's federal, state, and city income tax returns for consistency and propriety of reporting. Next year, you'll receive a personalized

organizer with prior year amounts shown for comparison purposes.

3. Upon receipt of your tax organizer packet, we ask that you take one specific action: please review, sign, and return to us the engagement agreement, which sets forth the terms of our services as your tax preparer.
4. After you have completed the organizer, feel free to call our office to arrange for a personal interview with the professional staff person or partner assigned to prepare your return. Many clients choose to merely mail us their data when ready. Others prefer the opportunity to sit down face-to-face with us to review their data and discuss other issues they have regarding tax compliance and estate, tax, business, or financial planning items.
5. If we receive your information after April 5, 20YY, we may not be able to meet the April 15 deadline, and an extension may be necessary. If you are missing information, such as a K-1 from a partnership, S corporation, estate, or trust, we suggest that an appointment be made before you receive all that information so that we can get started. You can provide the K-1s separately when you receive them.
6. If you know you will be getting an extension, an appointment may still be necessary in order to determine how much is owed by April 15, 20YY. You may wish to also address first quarter estimates for 20YY at that time.
7. Finally, if you have children, especially if they are under age 18 and have interest and dividend income, or if you have sold a security in their name, you might need to file returns for them. Please let us know this in the event we have to file for an extension for them.

If you know anyone you would like us to provide a blank organizer to, please do not hesitate to call us.

Thank you so very much for your attention to these important details. We sincerely appreciate your assistance; cooperation; and, of course, your patronage.

Sincerely,

ABO AND COMPANY, LLC

Letter Sent With Organizer for a New Client

Welcome New Clients,

Thank you for allowing us to be of service to you in preparing your personal tax returns and attending to your overall tax and financial planning needs. Business is great, but we're always excited to service new and interesting clients.

Enclosed is our tax return organizer.

Don't panic!

We use this method to help clients organize their information and make our professional time and resultant fees most productive. Although it's blank this first year, starting next year, our computer generated organizer will have the prior year's information printed for easy comparison. Professional fees are a function of the professional time expended on your behalf at our standard billing rates, plus any associated costs. Rates currently span from $XXX per hour for partners to $XX–$XXX per hour for staff time, depending on experience.

When you believe you have accumulated the substantial portion of your tax information, hopefully with the assistance of the organizer, please give us a call so that we can set up a mutually convenient time to meet.

Do the best you can, jotting down any questions or highlighting areas you think worthy of discussing with us.

We're here for you!

Abo and Company, LLC

This letter was provided courtesy of Martin Abo of Abo and Company, LLC, Voorhees, NJ.

Organizer and Forms from Vision Financial Group CPAs, LLP

January 12, 20XX

Dear Client:

On behalf of Vision Financial Group CPAs, LLP, we would like to extend our warmest wishes for a healthy and happy new year.

Enclosed, you will find a return envelope addressed to Vision Financial Group CPAs, LLP, for you to forward to us your 20WW tax documents. If you have any tax questions, please contact Michael Slotopolsky or Jacob Ansel at 1-XXX-XXX-XXXX.

It would be advantageous for you to send in your documents as soon as possible. This will enable our firm to expedite your 20WW tax return.

Enclosed you will find a 1040 checklist, which will assist you with the tax documents we will need in order to complete your 20WW tax return. Please sign the enclosed engagement letter and return it to us with your tax documents in the envelope provided.

Thank you in advance.

Sincerely,

Michael Slotopolsky, CPA

Managing Partner

Jacob Ansel, CPA

Partner

Engagement Letter From Vision Financial Group CPAs, LLP

Dear________________________,

We will prepare the following tax returns for the year ended December 31, 20WW:

- Federal income tax return—Form 1040
- State income tax return(s)
- City income tax return(s) (if applicable)

It is your responsibility to provide us with all of the necessary information to complete your tax return. In that regard, you state that, to the best of your knowledge and belief you have provided us true, correct, and complete information regarding amounts you have claimed as tax deductions and have maintained written documentation supporting all amounts, including log books and receipts. You understand that taxing authorities may examine the returns; that documentation should be retained to support the information provided to us, especially business travel and entertainment deductions, business use percentage of autos and other assets, barter activities, and the required documents to support charitable contributions of $250 or more; and that penalties may be imposed on returns that are late, underpaid, or incorrect and that deductions might be disallowed if you are audited and are unable to provide the proper substantiation to support the amounts claimed as a deduction.

We will not audit or otherwise verify any information. We may require clarification or additional information. We are not responsible for disallowed deductions; the inclusion of additional unreported income; or any resulting taxes, penalties, or interest.

You understand that you will be charged an additional fee if we are asked to assist or represent you in a tax examination or respond to a tax agency inquiry or notice.

You will contact us immediately if you discover additional information that will lead to a change in your return or if you receive any letters from the IRS or state or local tax authorities.

Our policy is to put all tax advice in writing; therefore, you cannot rely upon any unwritten advice because it may be tentative, incomplete, or not fully reviewed.

Initial_______

We will use our judgment to resolve questions in your favor when a tax law is unclear or if there is a reasonable justification for doing so. Whenever we are aware that applicable tax law is unclear or that there are conflicting interpretations of the law by authorities, we will explain the possible positions that may be taken on your return. We will follow whatever position you request, so long as it is consistent with the codes, regulations, and interpretations that have been promulgated by the U.S. government. If the IRS later contests the position taken, there may be an assessment of additional tax, plus interest and penalties. We assume no liability for any such additional penalties or assessments.

If you expect us to perform other services or tax returns, such as estate, gift, sales, fiduciary, property, states, or locals, please note them at the bottom of this letter.

Record Retention

In accordance with our firm's current document retention policy, we will retain digitally our working papers, selected copies of your documents that were considered or used in the preparation of your return, and your tax returns for your engagement for seven years. We will provide you a copy of the depreciation schedules and tax returns and other pertinent working papers that should be a part of your books and records. If you need replacements, we will provide additional copies at our standard copying fees. All of your original records will be returned to you. After seven years, our working papers and files will no longer be available. Physical deterioration or catastrophic events may shorten the time during which our records will be available. The working papers and files of our firm are not substitutes for the original records. It is agreed and understood that in connection with the performance of this engagement by Vision Financial Group CPAs, LLP, the working papers we prepare shall remain the property of Vision Financial Group CPAs, LLP.

Attorney Fees

If any disputes arise among the parties, they agree to try first in good faith to settle the dispute by mediation administered by the American Arbitration Association (AAA) under its Commercial Mediation Rules. All unresolved disputes shall then be decided by final and binding arbitration, in accordance with the Commercial Arbitration Rules of the AAA. Fees charged by any mediators, arbitrators, or the AAA shall be shared equally by all parties. In agreeing to arbitration, we both acknowledge that in the event of a dispute over fees, each of us is giving up the right to have the dispute decided in a court of law before a judge or jury and, instead, are accepting the use of arbitration for resolution.

Initial______

We appreciate the opportunity to serve you and look forward to a continuing, mutually satisfying relationship.

Very truly yours,

Vision Financial Group CPAs, LLP

The terms described in the letter are acceptable, are hereby agreed to, and shall remain in effect until terminated by either party in writing.

Accepted by:_____________________ Date:__________

Please sign and return all pages.

Please check how you would like to receive your tax return for 20WW:

_____Paper copy and original documents

_____CD copy of tax return and original documents

_____CD copy of tax return and CD of original documents

_____Through our secure client portal

SAMPLE ENGAGEMENT LETTER FROM ABO AND COMPANY:

CONDITIONS OF THIS ENGAGEMENT

The purpose of this letter is to confirm our understanding of the terms and objectives of our engagement to prepare your 20XX individual income tax returns and to clarify the nature and limitations of the services you have requested of Abo and Company, LLC.

We will prepare 20XX federal and state income returns with information you furnish to us. We will not be responsible for the preparation of any other returns or forms unless specifically directed to do so by you.

1. You are confirming to us that you will furnish us with all information required for the timely preparation of your income tax returns or, in the event extensions of time for filing are necessary, the information that may be required to enable us to reasonably estimate the tax payable with the extension request. We request that you provide us with your tax information no later than April 1, 20YY, so that we can complete your returns by the April 15th deadline. We will make every effort to accommodate you. If your information is not received by that time, however, it is our normal policy to extend returns that are not complete to allow us time for proper review. If your return is not completed by April 15, 20YY, you may be subject to late filing or late payment penalties.
2. You are representing to us that the information you supply is accurate and complete to the best of your knowledge and supported by adequate records as required by law. We will not audit or otherwise verify the information that you give us although we may ask for clarification of some of the items. By your signature at the end of this engagement, you

are confirming to us that—unless we are otherwise advised—the travel, entertainment, gifts, and all deductions are supported by the necessary records required under the Internal Revenue Code. If you have any questions regarding the type of records required, please ask us. You are authorizing us to use our judgment in determining your tax information's most appropriate presentation. You also understand that in signing the return(s), you accept responsibility for the information's accuracy, documentation, and proper presentation. All such documentation should be retained by you in the event of a federal, state, or local audit. Recent changes to the tax code require disclosure of certain foreign assets. You must inform us if you think this may apply to your tax situation. We strongly suggest you review the special posting on our website for further information, www.aboandcompany.com.

3. In accumulating information for the income tax returns, please be aware of the Internal Revenue Service's and state substantiation requirements. Regulations require you to maintain and retain information substantiating items reported on your returns. Should you have any questions as to what documentation will satisfy the taxing authorities' rules we will be pleased to advise you regarding proper documentation on a case-by-case basis. We assume no liability for any additional penalties or assessments relating to your failure to meet these requirements and suggest you keep these records for a minimum of seven years.
4. Your returns are subject to examination by taxing authorities. In the event of an audit, you may be requested to produce documents, records, or other evidence to substantiate the items of income and deduction shown on tax returns. Any items that are not resolved in your favor by the examiner are

subject to certain rights of appeal. If an examination of your return(s) occurs, we will represent you if requested. However, these additional services are not included in our regular fees for preparation of tax returns. Although we are available to provide you with tax planning advice, we are not obligated to do so unless you specifically request it. You should not necessarily rely on any informal discussions or unwritten advice because it may be tentative and not yet fully reviewed.

5. It is important for you to know that the law provides for an "accuracy" penalty to be imposed where a taxpayer makes a substantial understatement of their tax liability. The penalty is 20 percent of the tax underpayment. Taxpayers may seek to avoid all or part of the penalty by showing (1) that they acted in good faith and there was reasonable cause for the understatement, (2) that the understatement was based on substantial authority, or (3) that the relevant facts affecting the items' tax treatment were adequately disclosed on the return.
6. We prepare tax returns with the aid of an in-house computer system and generally provide clients with a 20XX Tax Organizer. If you have not received it, please ask us for one. Please fill in the 20XX amounts on the appropriate lines and answer the questions as completely as possible. This will aid us in preparing a complete and accurate return and allow us to keep our fees to a minimum. Make notations as needed for any information that has changed since last year and for any new items of income, expense deduction, or credit not reported in your prior year return.
7. We will also need your 20XX W-2 and 1099 forms, copies of any real estate closing statements, any K-1 schedules (received from partnerships, S corporations, LLCs, and so on), and other similar

information. Please keep your completed organizer with your 20XX information. If there is any question about a particular document, we encourage you to bring it to us or call us.

8. Professional standards now require us to electronically file all federal and state individual income tax returns ("e-filing"). However, you do have the right to "opt out" of the e-filing program. Please notify our firm immediately should you desire not to have your return e-filed, so that we may provide you with the form(s) necessary for opting out of the e-file program. Please note that unless you notify us of your desire to not e-file your return, we will prepare your return to be e-filed.
9. Although e-filing requires both you and our firm to complete additional steps, the same filing deadlines will apply. You must therefore ensure that you complete the additional requirements well before the due dates in order for our firm to be able to timely transmit your return. We will provide you with a paper copy of the income tax returns for your review prior to electronic transmission. After you have reviewed the returns, you must provide us with a signed authorization indicating that you have reviewed the return and that, to the best of your knowledge, you feel it is correct. We cannot transmit the returns to the taxing authorities until we have such authorization. Therefore, if you have not provided our firm with your signed authorization, we may need to place your return on extension, even though it might already have been completed. In that event, you will be responsible for ensuring that any payment due with the extension is timely sent to the appropriate taxing authorities. You will also be responsible for any additional costs our firm incurs arising from the extension preparation.

10. Please note that although our firm will use our best efforts to ensure that your returns are successfully transmitted to the appropriate taxing authorities, we will not be financially responsible for electronic transmission or other errors arising after your return has been successfully submitted from our office.
11. It is our policy to keep records related to this engagement for seven years. However, we do not keep original client records so we will return those to you at the completion of the services rendered under this engagement. When records are returned to you, it is your responsibility to retain and protect your records for possible future use, including potential examination by any government or regulatory agencies.
12. If this engagement involves a joint return, this firm will supply a copy upon request at any time to either taxpayer without obtaining the additional consent of the other party. A retrieval or copying charge may apply.
13. Our fees for these services will be at our standard rates for the time spent, plus computer processing charges. Payment is expected upon delivery of your tax returns. If you have any complaints, claimed errors, discrepancies or objections to a statement, you should notify us within 30 days of the invoicing although our maximum liability to you arising from services under this letter is limited to the fees you pay for these services. In the event outstanding invoices are placed in the hands of an attorney or collection agency for collection, whether suit is instituted or not, there shall be due from you, in addition to the outstanding balance, all costs and expenses incurred by us for the collection and payment of reasonable attorneys' fees or other costs of collection.

14. If any dispute arises between you and Abo and Company, we agree first to try in good faith to settle the dispute by mediation administered by the American Arbitration Association under its Rules for Professional Accounting and Related Services Disputes before resorting to litigation. The costs of any mediation proceeding shall be shared equally by us. The mediation shall be conducted in Abo and Company, LLC's resident county and state. Failure to respond to requests for mediation may result in proceeding directly to arbitration as described in the following paragraph and if the Mediation has not been requested by you within 90 days of any invoice, we may proceed directly to arbitration.
15. Abo and Company and you agree that any dispute over fees and costs charged by the accountant to you will be submitted for resolution by arbitration in accordance with the rules for professional accounting and related services disputes of the American Arbitration Association. Such arbitration shall be binding and final. This provision shall only apply to disputes arising from fees charged by us. In the event you want to assert a counterclaim in the arbitration, we must consent in writing to allow such counterclaim and reserve the right to deny such a request. In agreeing to arbitration, we both acknowledge that, in the event of a dispute over fees charged by us, we each are giving up the right to have the dispute decided in a court of law before a judge or jury and instead are accepting arbitration for resolution of fee disputes. Claims arising under the services provided pursuant to this letter shall be decided using Abo and Company, LLC's state law.
16. In the event we are required by subpoena or other legal process to produce documents, work product, client papers or materials or any other portions of

the files or information maintained by us for you or on your behalf, you agree to pay any costs associated with the production including, but not limited to, storage retrieval costs, copying costs, our costs of administration in looking for, retrieving, reviewing and producing the information or documents requested as well as any attorney fees incurred by us. Upon receipt of a subpoena or other process for documents and information, we will send such subpoena or process to you via regular mail at the last known address we have for you. It will be your responsibility to file such motions or objections to the requested production. If you do not obtain an appropriate order or stay of the subpoena, we will produce the documents. If we are required to appear in court, arbitration hearing, deposition or other hearing you will pay the hourly rate or rates of the person or persons in our accounting firm required to appear.

We are pleased to have you as a client and sincerely appreciate being of service to you. Our objective is to provide the highest level of professional service, delivered on a timely basis at a competitive cost. It is of the utmost importance for us to know at all times that you are satisfied with the professional services provided. To ensure full communication between us and a clear understanding and prompt resolution with any concerns you may have about our services, you agree to let us know immediately of any concerns you may have about the services being performed or invoices rendered.

If it is agreed that the foregoing sets forth the conditions of the engagement of Abo and Company, LLC by you, please sign this letter in the space provided and return it promptly. We may not release your returns until this is returned to our files. If there are other tax returns you expect us to prepare, such as sales, gift, intangible or local (or both), please inform us by noting at the end of this letter.

Abo and Company, LLC

By signing below, the client acknowledges that he or she has provided information required for the preparation of the income returns that is true, correct, and complete to the best of his or her knowledge; has read the engagement agreement; has received a copy of the agreement; and understands and agrees to terms thereof.

Approved:__________________________ __________

Client's Signature Date

____

Please Print Name Here

EXHIBIT 5-2 Sample Organizer Cover Letter—Long Version

January 20XX

[Client Name]
[Client Address]

Dear [Client Name],

The time for filing your 20YY federal and state individual income tax returns is approaching. In order to assist you in gathering the necessary information, we have enclosed your 20YY tax organizer. It is designed to help you organize the information that we will need to prepare your income tax returns.

If there are items that are not clear to you, please note them, and we will review those items with you. However, it would be helpful if you completed as much of the organizer as possible. This will facilitate the preparation of your income tax returns. Following, we have listed some hints that should help you provide the documents that we will need to prepare your tax returns.

Hints on How to Compile Your Tax Information

<u>Names and Social Security Numbers</u>

Please make sure that all Social Security numbers reported on the return (you, spouse, and dependents) are correct and that the names exactly match the Social Security cards. The IRS will disallow exemptions and certain credits if there is a mismatch. Please contact the Social Security Administration if there is a problem.

<u>Salary</u>

We need all parts of all of your W-2 forms.

<u>Interest and Dividends</u>

Provide us with all 1099 forms you have received. If you earned interest or dividend income from a particular investment but did not receive a Form 1099, please contact the institution for the missing information. In the meantime, please give us the amount that should be reported.

If you receive tax-exempt interest, we need to know the amount and the source of this income. Tax-exempt interest is required to be reported (even though it is not taxable) to the federal government and, in some cases, to state taxing authorities. Also, some type of tax exempt interest is subject to the Alternative Minimum Tax.

Social Security and Unemployment Insurance

We need to know the full amount of Social Security and unemployment insurance benefits received. Provide us with the 1099s for those items.

Pension, Profit Sharing, and IRAs

Please indicate the dates and amounts of any payments made into an IRA, Roth IRA, simplified employee pension (SEP) plan, Keogh plan, or SIMPLE IRA and the year for which you wish to claim the deduction.

If you received distributions from an IRA or pension, profit sharing, SEP, 401(k), or 403(b) plans, please provide us with Forms 1099-R or W2-P, or both. If any of these amounts were rolled over into another plan or an IRA, please give us the details.

If you converted an IRA to a Roth IRA, please provide the information. If you wish to reconvert back to a traditional IRA, please call us to discuss.

Income From Partnerships, S Corporations, Limited Liability Companies, Estate, and Trusts

Please furnish all Schedules K-1 and accompanying statements of additional information received from these entities.

Sales of Securities

In the event you sold stocks, bonds, or other securities during the year, we will need brokerage statements reflecting the capital gains and losses or copies of buy and sell confirmation slips. If you maintained a brokerage account, please provide us with copies of the monthly statements, as well as the year-end statement (including Form 1099B).

Regarding mutual funds and other securities sold, please note that it is your responsibility to provide us with the cost basis, including the effect of any reinvested dividends. Many mutual funds can now furnish you that information. If you ask us to do these computations, we will charge an additional fee.

If you sold securities you inherited or received as a gift, obtain the cost basis from the executor or donor.

Sales or Purchase of Real Estate

If real estate was sold or purchased during the year, furnish us a copy of the closing statements. If you sold your residence or other real property, we need to know your cost basis, as well as the cost of improvements made during your ownership. Also, give us a copy of Form 1099-S.

Business Income or Rental Real Estate

Summarize your gross receipts. We suggest that you review deposits made in your business and personal bank accounts to insure that all income was properly included in your summary. Expenses should be summarized by type of expenditure (for example, telephone, electricity, repairs, commissions, travel, and entertainment). Meals and entertainment, which are subject to a 50 percent limitation, should not be combined with other expense items.

If you are not presently maintaining a formal set of accounting books and records, we can suggest an inexpensive user-friendly computer software system to cut down the time it takes to record and summarize your records. If you maintain your transactions on Quicken, Money, or any other software program, it might be easier if you e-mail your file to us. Please speak to us to determine the best way to proceed.

NJ Residents' Homestead and NJ Saver Rebates

Please provide us with the amount received, which must be subtracted from your federal real estate tax deduction if your return utilizes itemized deductions.

Deductions

We suggest that you make a preliminary review of the lists of deductions contained in the organizer and provide us with a summary of your deductible amounts.

Also summarize the cash expenses noted in your travel and expense diary (see the following).

When completed, record the totals on the appropriate page of the organizer.

If you do not know whether a particular expense is tax deductible, please identify it for us so that we can discuss it with you.

State and Local Sales Tax Deduction

Taxpayers have the choice to deduct the greater of state and local income taxes or state and local sales taxes. If you live in a state that does not have state and local income taxes, the sales tax deduction will probably apply to you. Most taxpayers will still benefit most by utilizing the state and local income tax deduction. If the sales tax deduction applies to you, you do not have to gather all of your sales tax receipts. The IRS has published tables for the sales tax deduction, which are based on your income. Sales tax for major purchases, such as automobiles and boats, is allowed, in addition to the table amounts. If in doubt, please provide us with the documents for your major purchases.

Business Entertainment and Meals

Entertainment and meal expenses are only 50 percent deductible. You should separate your business expenses into the following categories:

1. Hotel room charges (fully deductible)
2. Meals, including those incurred while away from home (50 percent deductible)
3. Entertainment costs (50 percent deductible)
4. Transportation costs (fully deductible)

Please note that expenses under $75 per item that are properly and timely entered in a diary do not have to be substantiated with receipts. However, for all items of meals and entertainment, the amount, time and place, date, business purpose, and business relationship must be recorded in the diary, on the receipt, or on some other expense record.

Charitable Contributions

Please note that most cash charitable contributions need to be substantiated by a receipt or letter from the organization. For contribution transactions of $250 or more, you must obtain a contemporaneous written acknowledgement from the charitable organization. If you have not obtained such documentation, you must do so by April 15 or you are not permitted to take the deduction. You do not need to provide us with the receipts, but you must maintain them in the event of an audit. If you have not obtained the receipts but expect to, we can file an extension and then file your return when you have the proper substantiation. Let us know.

We will need a listing of any property you donated and the original cost or other basis of that property. If you contributed property, other than publicly traded securities, with a total claimed value over $5,000, you must obtain a qualified appraisal. Provide us with a copy that we could include with your tax return.

20YY Estimated Tax Payments

You must provide us with copies of cancelled checks (or bank statement entries) for all federal, state, and city estimated tax payments that have been made for tax year 20YY. Please note that the final estimated tax payments could have been made in January 20XX. In addition, in some instances, we will be checking directly with the IRS and state tax authorities to verify all estimated tax payments. In order to do so, we must have any postcards received from these agencies, which contain your personal identification numbers (PINs). The preceding procedures are necessary in order to prevent the issuance of tax notices and the resulting assessment of additional taxes, interest, and penalties.

20XX Estimated Tax

We will normally prepare 20XX estimates on the basis of your income and withholding taxes for 20YY. We will use the best procedure that minimizes the possibility of a penalty for underpayment of estimated tax. If you anticipate a significant change in your income for 20XX or a change in your withholding taxes, please advise us when you submit your tax data. If your income should change later in the year, please advise us at that time, and we will determine if your estimates require an amendment.

Hope and Lifetime Learning Credits

If you, your spouse, or your dependents attended college or another postsecondary educational institution, you may be entitled to a credit on your tax return. Please provide us with the details and any forms received from the institution verifying attendance and the amount of tuition. Please note that based on the amount of your adjusted gross income, you might not qualify. If you are married filing separately, you will not qualify, regardless of your income.

Gift Taxes

Making gifts of assets does not generally save income taxes but can drastically reduce eventual estate taxes. In some situations, capital gains taxes can also be transferred to the gift recipient. We should be apprised of all gifts to individuals over $14,000, as well as all gifts, whatever the amount, to trusts that include or can include grandchildren. We can then discuss the income, gift, and estate tax aspects with you.

Joint Versus Separate Returns

It usually is better for married couples to file joint returns. However, in certain instances, it might be better or advisable to file separately. This would include situations when one spouse owes large amounts to the IRS or for child support, there are marital difficulties, there are dual residency or second home issues, or there is the incidence of certain deductions for one spouse and not the other. Please advise us of any special circumstances that you think we should consider when we prepare your return.

If you file separately, and the reason for that filing subsequently changes, you can refile jointly within the three year statute of limitations. Once you file jointly, you are precluded from filing separately.

Amended Returns

It may happen that when you prepare for the filing of your 20YY tax return, you find an error on a previously filed tax return. Please let us know as soon as possible. Amended returns can be filed for the last three years up until April 15, 20XX (and possibly later if you had an extension for a prior year).

Electronic Filing

We plan to electronically file your 20YY federal and state individual income tax returns, whenever possible. Electronic filing provides definite benefits to you, including reduction of processing errors by the tax authorities, faster refunds (usually within 10–14 days), fewer (or no) documents to sign, no envelopes to mail, and confirmation to us that your tax returns were received by the tax authorities. We will provide you with an IRS e-file signature authorization after we complete your returns. This will allow us to electronically file your return with your electronic signature in the form of a PIN. You can also pay balances due by check, direct debit from your bank account, or credit card. We suggest that you send us a voided copy of a check from your checking account when you forward your tax information to us. This will provide us with the proper banking information for direct deposit tax refunds (the fastest way to get your refund) or electronic payment of balances due (which can be scheduled to occur anytime up to April 15).

Preparation Process for Your Tax Returns

Preparing your tax returns accurately and efficiently is very important to us. The procedure for your tax returns may involve outsourcing parts of the preparation process in order to improve client service and turnaround time, as well as manage costs. Every income tax return completed by us undergoes a quality review by one of our firm's tax professionals and is approved and signed by one of our partners.

IRS Correspondence

There are now checkboxes authorizing the IRS and most state tax authorities to discuss any problems in processing the tax returns directly with your preparer, eliminating the need for extra correspondence and having to obtain power of attorney forms. We recommend that you authorize such discussions by checking the appropriate box in your organizer. If you do not check this box in the negative, we will assume you will want the tax authorities to contact us directly in the event of any questions. Of course, we will never agree to anything that will cost you additional taxes, interest, or penalties without your assent.

Conclusion

We rely on you to provide us with complete and accurate tax return information. This will allow us to prepare your returns expeditiously. In addition, your tax return will be better able to withstand scrutiny by the IRS and other taxing authorities. When your information package is complete, please submit it to us as soon as possible. If you are missing only a few items, such as a Schedule K-1, please do not delay. We can get started and add the additional information when you receive it.

Should you have any questions about the information we need to prepare your tax returns, please call our office.

Cordially,

[***Partner Signature***]

P.S. If you would like to discuss as any aspects of your personal financial planning, please either indicate that when you send in your tax information or call us to discuss how we can help you.

EXHIBIT 5-3 Sample E-File Procedures Information Sheet

E-File Procedures

Client Information Sheet

If your tax returns qualify, both federal and state returns will be e-filed. This will enable you to get your refund (if any) faster, avoid IRS processing problems and errors that may be encountered in transcribing your returns, and eliminate the need to go to the post office to file your returns.

Unless you notify us that you do not want to e-file your returns by answering "No" to question 15 in the organizer, they will be processed for e-filing.

The e-filing process is quite simple and will entail the following:

- When your returns are completed, we will send you your copy of the returns to review and approve, together with forms that will authorize us to e-file your returns.
- Once you have approved the returns for e-filing, please sign the forms where indicated (if filing a joint return, both spouses must sign) and return them to us in the envelope provided. Alternatively, you can fax the forms to us at 1-XXX-XXX-XXXX. These forms will not only provide us with your consent to e-file the returns but will act as your electronic signature on the e-filed returns. Upon our receipt of your signed forms, we will e-file your returns.
- Your tax refund can be expedited by having it directly deposited into your account. This can be accomplished by supplying us with your bank's routing number and your account number and indicating whether the account is a savings or checking account. To ensure that the proper numbers are entered, please send us a copy of a voided check. This information should be supplied to us on the bottom of the "Taxpayer Information" page of the organizer.

- If you have a balance due to the U.S. Treasury or the state of New Jersey, you can pay it in one of three ways:
  - *By check.* We will send you vouchers to remit payment to the U.S. Treasury and the state of New Jersey. Even though your return has been e-filed before April 15, payments can be made with vouchers that are mailed in time to reach the IRS and the state of New Jersey by April 15.
  - *By credit card.* You can use American Express, Visa, MasterCard, or Discover Card to pay your tax liability. A convenience charge is charged by the service provider for this service. For federal returns, contact Official Payments Corporation (1-800-2PAY-TAX or www.officialpayments.com) or Link2Gov Corporation (1-888-PAY-1040 or www.pay1040.com). For New Jersey returns contact Official Payments Corporation at 1-888-PAY-1040.
  - *By electronic funds withdrawal or electronic check.* If you request electronic funds withdrawal for the federal return, we will enter the withdrawal date of April 13 to assure that the tax is timely paid. The same information requested for direct deposit will be used for the electronic funds withdrawal. For New Jersey, you can use an e-check by going to their website at www.state.nj.us/treasury/taxation/ or calling the state at 1-609-292-6400.

Unless we are notified otherwise, we will send you payment vouchers with your copy of the tax returns. Please note, we will not send out reminder notices with regard to the timely mailing of the payments and vouchers to the U.S. Treasury and the state of New Jersey.

EXHIBIT 5-4 Information Checklist Sent to Clients

1040 Information Checklist

This is a list of the most common items we'll need to finish your returns. We'll call you if we need anything else. (You don't need to return this list to us unless you make notes we should be aware of.)

- All return packets or mailing labels sent to you by the various taxing agencies.
- All W-2s.
- All 1099 forms received confirming income from interest, dividends, retirement, Social Security, disability, unemployment, gambling winnings, and so on.
- All income information for children if you want us to prepare any required returns.
- Year-end statement of mortgage interest (Form 1098), escrow activity, and balance on mortgage or home equity loans and real estate taxes paid.
- Total of charitable contributions and details for any noncash contributions over $500.
- Copies of all LLC, partnership, S corporation or Trust K-1s (send separately later if everything else is ready, and let us know they're coming).
- A closing statement for each transaction if you bought, sold, or refinanced real estate.
- If you sold any shares of mutual funds and basis information is not provided by the broker, detail all activity in the funds sold from original purchase date through date-of-sale date (year-end summary statements are ideal).
- If you are claiming auto mileage as a deduction for business, rental properties, or unreimbursed employee expenses, we need to know total miles, commuting miles, and business miles driven for the year.

- If you lease your car or are deducting actual expenses, please also provide the original value of the car (what you could have bought it for); the date of lease; and all expenses for lease payments, gas, car washes, licenses, insurance, tires, repairs, and so on.
- Copies of any federal, state, or local tax correspondence during the year, including all payments made or refunds received.
- All legal documents for divorce decrees.
- Voided check for the account where refunds should be direct deposited (optional).
- Signed engagement letter (see attached).
- **New clients:** copies of prior federal, state, and local returns and depreciation schedules, if applicable (at least one year, preferably three).
- Copies of cancelled checks or other proof of payment for all federal and state estimated tax payments (all quarters paid).

This document is provided courtesy of Vision Financial Group CPAs LLC, Morganville, NJ.

Tax Notice Service Letter

Tax notices are coming with increasing frequency. Fees for handling such notices are getting higher and higher, especially with the nonresponsiveness of some tax agency personnel.

Rather than bill each client as work is done, you can institute a process in which you add a fixed amount to each client's tax return fee and then handle any notices without additional charge.

A sample letter to notify clients of this service is included as exhibit 5-5, "Sample Tax Notice Service Letter."

EXHIBIT 5-5 Sample Tax Notice Service Letter

January 20XX

[Client Name]
[Client Address]

Dear [Client Name],

Of late, there has been an epidemic of individual tax notices and inquiries from the IRS and the state tax authorities. These notices usually result from a mistake by the tax agency, income reported to the tax agency for which the taxpayer didn't receive the appropriate information documents, or incorrect estimated tax payments.

Should you receive a tax notice, it makes sense for you to forward it to us to check it out. We normally charge extra for this service. As you may know, the fees for individual services are becoming quite expensive, sometimes more than the cost of the actual tax return. This is not through the fault of our clients or us but, rather, is the nature of dealing with the "new" IRS and the state tax authorities.

In order to institute a more equitable process and spread the costs, we have initiated a policy under which we will charge every individual tax client a $XXX fee for each tax year, which will cover any notices or inquiries for tax returns we have prepared. In this manner, nobody will be charged extra if and when a tax notice occurs.

Please note that the tax notice service fee referred to previously does not apply to tax examinations, meetings with tax agents or collections officers, extensive phone calls, and appeals (which would be billed at our standard hourly rates). Generally, our contact with you under the tax notice service does not include any meetings but would involve telephone, fax, or e-mail.

If you have any questions about this new policy, please call us.

If you do not wish to participate in our tax notice service, please sign the following waiver and return it to our office within 10 days.

Sincerely,

[***Partner Signature***]

By checking this box I hereby acknowledge that I am declining the tax notice service. I understand that I will not be billed the $XXX fee for this service with my 20XX tax return, but if I ask you to respond to a tax notice, I will be charged at your standard hourly rates.

Name (please print)______ Signature______ Date_____

Privacy Notification

If you are not a CPA or attorney, every client for whom you prepare a tax return must be notified annually regarding your privacy policy. Some firms mail out the notice each year on a fixed date. Others mail it out with the tax organizers or completed tax return. Still others attach it to their engagement letters.

Consent to Disclosure of Tax Return Information

Federal law requires written consent before tax return information can be disclosed to third parties for purposes other than the preparation and filing of a tax return. Following is a sample form a client should complete before you disclose any taxpayer information.

DISCLOSURE LTR

Sample Form—Consent to Disclosure of Tax Return Information

Federal law requires this consent form to be provided to you. Unless authorized by law, we cannot disclose, without your consent, your tax return information to third parties for purposes other than the preparation and filing of your tax return. If you consent to disclosure of your tax return information, federal law may not protect your tax return information from further use or distribution.

You are not required to complete this form. If we obtain your signature on this form by conditioning our services on your consent, your consent will not be valid. If you agree to the disclosure of your tax return information, your consent is valid for the amount of time that you specify. If you do not specify the duration of your consent, your consent is valid for one year.

Please complete:

Purpose for forwarding information:_______________

Name and address to whom the information is being disclosed:

Duration of consent:_________________________

I, ________________, authorize (CPA firm) ________ ______________________ to disclose to the previously stated person my tax return information for _____ (tax year).

Signature:______________________________________

Date:____

If you believe your tax return information has been disclosed or used improperly in a manner unauthorized by law without your permission, you may contact the Treasury Inspector General for Tax Administration.

Implement a Staff Tax Training Program 6

Training is important to ensure as accurate a return as possible. It is also important as a tool to establish as much uniformity throughout the office as possible. Uniformity will enable staff to help each other, make it possible to have someone not familiar with a file to complete a return with missing information or make changes or review the return, and establish a consistency of work throughout the firm.

We put tremendous effort and energy into staff training. In effect, training is continuous, with each person expected to learn, develop, and grow professionally and technically. We also place great emphasis on procedure compliance. Our lives are always made better when things are done correctly. It makes review, error disclosure, and training easier and a pleasure, rather than a chore.

We focus on two types of training: the pre-tax-season meeting and on-the-job (OTJ) training. This chapter discusses both of these and includes a section on maintaining morale.

The Pre-Tax-Season Meeting

For tax season, the kickoff is our annual pre-tax-season meeting, held from 5:00 P.M. to 9:30 P.M. over a buffet dinner during the first week of February. We have a 200-plus page manual that contains the procedures we want followed during tax season, a section on tax changes that we want to highlight, copies of our internal forms, and an organizer and tax information for a sample client whose return will be prepared that evening.

The staff meeting consists of three separate parts:

- Part 1 is a discussion of tax law changes and highlights and our procedures and processes. This lasts approximately 100 minutes.
- Part 2 is the preparation of a sample tax return on IRS forms. This lasts approximately 100 minutes.

- Part 3 is a discussion and critique of the return. This lasts approximately 50 minutes.

We allow 20 minutes for eating, even though we work through dinner. We give five continuing professional education credits.

Part of our training that has been successful for us is for the staff to prepare a sample return on government forms, followed by a discussion of the results. We have enhanced this program by customizing the preparation to the preparer's level. Proctors walk around supervising the preparation, and each person fills in the parts of the return geared toward his or her level, with everyone actually calculating the taxable income and the income tax. Filled-in forms for the parts that individuals did not manually prepare are handed out during the appropriate time in the preparation session.

We usually invite colleagues from other firms to join us. Doing so allows us to share information with them, as well as gain different perspectives, so we can all learn and grow. This part of the meeting has been very successful for everyone attending.

The objectives of our meeting are as follows:

- Create respect for tax season.
- Create morale and spirit.
- Strengthen our firm culture ("We are different, and we are better, and we work together.") and brand (what we stand for and the quality behind everything we do).
- Prepare a return on actual forms, so there will be a "feel" for returns.
- Ensure the highest quality of preparation at each level handling the return, starting with the lowest level.

OTJ Training

A key element of the success of the training is the reinforcement during actual return preparation. Our experience has taught us that the most effective method is OTJ training, not the classroom lecture. To work properly, the training has to be available, continuous, consistent, and reinforced. The overseers of OTJ training typically are the reviewers. Thus, the highest level trains the lowest.

A quick word about this training method: it is essential that a classroom-type training program be conducted. The staff has to be shown what to do, procedures to follow and how to get as much of the work done before seeking help, and how they can check their work and find their own errors. However, my experience has shown that most people will not follow what they are taught; they are impatient, have a short attention span, and are anxious to get to work on a return. For that reason, OTJ training has to be deliberate, focused, and consistent every time it is needed. It is essentially training by correcting errors. References can be made to what was taught in the classroom, but the direction has to come with the actual work. If the higher level staff do not follow through on OTJ training, there will be no growth, except by extremely bright or more motivated staff. The OTJ training program is not a replacement for classroom training; it is more regular and occurs almost daily, but the classroom training takes place before any of the work is attempted or started.

The tendency during the very busy time is for the reviewers to fix errors themselves in order to save time and move the return. Resisting this habit can be one of the hardest things to do; however, if the reviewer has the preparer fix the errors, it increases the probability that those errors won't be made again. In contrast, by making the changes himself or herself, the reviewer ensures the errors will likely be made every time the opportunity arises. Expediency has to step aside to meet the firm's goals and doing so has to be by clear, deliberate, consistent, and regular training, with error corrections an integral part of this training.

Tax season work compression is a time for long range thinking, but by some measure, the long term interests coincide directly with the short term. In tax season, two months of training and effort are concentrated into one week. Shortsightedness four days before April 15 can cause much more work for the reviewers and missed learning opportunities that cannot be reversed or made up. Dedication to training will pay long term dividends on all the errors avoided on the extended returns those preparers will be working on.

I have also found out that having the preparer make the changes teaches him or her what he or she did wrong and that he or she must be more careful because he or she is the one who will have to make the changes. Leaving the errors for the reviewer to correct is not a strategy that works.

Another element of the training is the availability of a go-to person a preparer can ask for assistance. This person can be the reviewer, another staff person, a manager, or even the engagement partner. Uniform procedures will aid the training because the methods and advice will be consistent and done in a consistent manner.

We also provide sensitivity training for error avoidance and to serve the client more efficiently. This practice requires the preparer to look at the finished return and try to project or understand how the client will react when he or she receives the return and the final bottom line. For example, if the final result is a large number (either a refund or payment), was the client previously made aware of this amount or will he or she be surprised; were unusual items on the return discussed with the client; are the client's dependents' names spelled correctly?

In summary, following are the key elements of the training:

1. OTJ training should be formalized, with consistent methods that are uniformly applied.
2. Develop methods so that everybody does everything the same way. Any one person should be able to pick up any other's work and proceed in the same way as the originating person.
3. Partners and senior staff have to become focused on the methodology and dedicated to the process of delegating, training, and developing.
4. You have to become a training organization.
5. Everybody you hire needs training. Even the most experienced people require training in your procedures, accountability, and oversight requirements. The inexperienced people need to be told everything, including how to turn on the computer and back up files. The experienced people might need procedures drummed into them even more than the new recruits in order to break some bad habits.
6. In training, we must find ways to constantly tell the staff they did a good job and to excite them, as well as to not let them go home upset or leave tasks unfinished.
7. Training methods should involve breaking jobs into smaller tasks. It's easier to get smaller things done right, and it's easier to review smaller things than big things. It also takes much less time to explain what to do for a short task than a large job.

8. Training should be done cheerfully and gracefully, not grudgingly.
9. The attitude should be to train and have the trainee do the tasks, not the trainer—who must avoid the attitude that it is easier for him or her to do the work.

Maintaining Morale

One of the problems we face from time to time, and we forget about it until it becomes a problem again, is to create a morale and spirit toward tax season. This should be worked at. Some firms have a pre-tax-season trip to a New York City museum, dinner, and show. During tax season, you can buy flowers and plants for your staff, get afternoon ice cream, vary the places from which you bring in lunch or dinner, close one Saturday, and occasionally let your staff go home earlier than 11:00 P.M. (just kidding).

Effectively Training New Employees[1]

A common issue notable in small businesses, including accounting firms, is how to efficiently and effectively train new employees. Each company and supervisor generally have their own way of doing things. However, as with all issues, some techniques work better than others.

I began my career at WithumSmith+Brown as an intern in January 2006. The training I received was direct, meaningful, and substantive. Those around me also had this type of training and mentorship, as evidenced by the fact that they are working by my side today and doing well. Now that I have been here for three years, I am transitioning from the protégée to the mentor and have adopted a couple of techniques from my previous managers and peers that I am applying to younger staff.

First, keeping a positive attitude is essential when working with new staff. If you portray apathy or act like work is not interesting and exciting, the staff will not be enthusiastic about learning. From the start, it is important to let the person you are training know that he or she should

[1] This section was written by Brad Caruso, CPA, a staff accountant at WithumSmith+Brown in 2009 when he had three years' experience. At the time of the publication of this third edition, Brad was a senior manager. The date references used here were kept in this section.

always communicate with you on any issue he or she encounters, even if it is something as small as forgetting your name. If a person does not feel comfortable talking to you, he or she generally will sit around and spend too much time trying to figure things out; whereas, if he or she knew to walk up to you, the problem would have been quickly solved.

Second, it is important to explain the task quickly and concisely. The average attention span of an entry-level staff member is generally three minutes, so if you add verbiage and stories and digress from what you want him or her to do, he or she will tune you out (not on purpose) or not understand what you assigned to him or her. One effective method is to explain an assignment in one minute and have the new employee repeat what you said. This will not only get him or her thinking, it will also give you a chance to clarify and refine your instructions and to ensure that he or she actually understands the task.

Third, it is important to properly motivate employees. Set realistic deadlines so they do not feel overwhelmed and so they have some guidance on the amount of time a task should take. Assigning short tasks generally is easier for both the assignor and assignee. Sometimes, giving the work in increments can be more effective than assigning a large task at once.

Finally, it is important to communicate results, so problems and issues can be resolved early and also so the employee can get satisfaction. Once the employee completes the task, explain how he or she did in comparison with your expected time frame, as well as the quality of his or her work. It is important to encourage employees and offer them praise for completing a task correctly.

Once you master the art of training employees (which I am working on every day), the company as a whole operates more efficiently and effectively. The training is taken from a higher level and passed to the younger staff, which helps them learn and allows them to start to take the role of trainer early on. Although training is not easy, the benefits that can be obtained from properly utilizing good practices are immense and innumerable.

Types of People Preparing Tax Returns

☑ Experienced

☑ Inexperienced

When inexperienced people are used

- whose job is it to train them?
- is training formal, dedicated, and consistent?
- is training uniformly applied when more than one person conducts the training?
- does the preparer know that he or she should recheck every return he or she worked on that is in the pipeline if an error is uncovered?
- is training haphazard and on the run when a person gets a return to work on?
- are errors corrected by the preparer rather than the reviewer?
- is the reviewer qualified to teach and review that level of return?
- is the tax return presented as an exciting growth opportunity or an infringement on the staff person's "important" assignments?
- does the firm have a culture of learning and training?

Staff Loyalty

Many firms expend great energy hiring and adding staff and then make no effort to excite them and make them feel part of the firm. Working at this takes almost no effort and yields superior results. Tax season is a perfect time to foster this feeling. Instead of assigning a list of returns to a staff person, show him or her the personal benefits of working on the individual returns of your clients. Following are nine benefits to staff:

- Lower level staff have an opportunity to speak to clients. In most business or larger assignments, the only people dealing directly with clients are the managers and partners. In contrast, for individual tax preparation work, it is not unusual for the staff person to call the client to get additional information, convey information, and also be the first person to whom the client addresses questions or shares a financial issue that is on his or her mind.

- The tax laws change on a fairly regular basis, creating a level playing field for knowledge of the new tax information. The least experienced staff member can know as much about the new laws as the most experienced staff member.
- When you meet people who possibly can become clients, or meet people who hear you are a CPA, they usually ask a tax question. Very few ask about a Financial Accounting Standards Board application. Working on tax returns arms you with ammunition to answer their questions.
- Taxes will lead you to the best opportunities to get new clients. This can be proven by tracing the family tree of your largest clients—many trace back to a 1040.
- Tax season is a relationship builder. It is not unusual for a staff person to interact with a couple of dozen clients during tax season. In a professional services firm, relationships are currency.
- Everyone knows about tax season, so you can get out of going to birthday parties for your spouse's cousin's in-laws' kids.
- Free dinners are provided for those working late.
- There is much less traffic when you go home after normal business hours.
- Tax season is fun. Because everyone is in the office at the same time, there is a team feeling and camaraderie as well as satisfaction of providing help and benefits to clients with their tax preparation.

Make staff aware of these advantages of tax season. To have engaged, excited staff, you have to engage and excite them.

TRACKING

Prepare a Preliminary Assignment Schedule 7

You should prepare a list of all returns by each due date. A printout should be given monthly (weekly during tax season) to each partner and in-charge staff person to use as a guide and checklist. You should include the type of return or service, the due date, updated status, and key people responsible for the return. A sample is included as exhibit 7-1, "Sample Tax Control Report by Due Date."

Additional information would be to include a code for a client group. We find it is helpful when we plan and work for a client to have a listing of every return we need to do for each client. It is also useful when we want the client to know everything we do for him or her and for clients to have a copy for themselves to be aware of and track due dates. A sample is included as exhibit 7-2, "Sample Tax Control Report by Client Group." There are many software programs that effectively have these schedules. There is also a new generation of work flow programs that many firms use that go much further than just tracking the dues dates—they track who has the return and the current status.

Items to consider when creating the schedule include the software used, how the schedule will be tracked, setting priorities, and the time needed to complete the return.

EXHIBIT 7-1 Sample Tax Control Report by Due Date

Client	*Client Group*	*Service or Return*	*Extended*	*Status*	*Key Person 1*	*Key Person 2*
Due Date: 11-15-XX						
A Corporation	7010023	1120	No	Sch	AA	BB
B Corporation	7020076	1120	Final	Rev	AA	CC
Due Date: 11-20-XX						
C Corporation	7010045	NJ ST115	N/A	Assigned	DD	
D Corporation	7190131	NJ ST115	N/A	Assigned	DD	
E Corporation	7030160	NY ST27	N/A	Assigned	EE	
Due Date: 11-23-XX						
Mr. and Mrs. F	7190131	Crummey Letter	N/A	Open	AA	Ptner 1

Due Date: 11-30-XX						
G Corporation	7190166	5500	Final	Assigned	EE	BB
Mr. and Mrs. F	7190131	Final tax projection for this year and preliminary for next year				
Due Date: 12-23-XX						
Mr. and Mrs. F	7190131	Life insurance premium pmt	N/A	Open	AA	Ptner 1

EXHIBIT 7-2

Sample Tax Control Report by Client Group

Client	*Client Group*	*Service or Return*	*Extended*	*Status*	*Key Person 1*	*Key Person 2*
Due Date: 3-15-XX						
G Corporation	7190131	1120			AA	BB
H Corporation	7190131	1120S			AA	CC
Due Date: 4-15-XX						
G Corporation	7190131	NJ CBT			DD	
H Corporation	7190131	NJ CBT-S			DD	
Mr. and Mrs. F	7190131	1040			EE	
Mr. and Mrs. F	7190131	NJ 1040				
Mr. F. Irrev Insurance Trust	7190131	1041				

F Family LLC	7190131	1065				
F Family LLC	7190131	NJ 1065				
F Charitable Foundation	7190131	Publish ad				
Due Date: 5-15-XX						
F Charitable Foundation	7190131	990-PF				
Due Date: 11-23-XX						
Mr. and Mrs. F	7190131	Crummey Letter			AA	

(continued)

Client	*Client Group*	*Service or Return*	*Extended*	*Status*	*Key Person 1*	*Key Person 2*
Due Date: 11-30-XX						
Mr. and Mrs. F	7190131	Final tax projection for this year and preliminary for next year				
Due Date: 12-23-XX						
Mr. and Mrs. F	7190131	Life insurance premium pmt			AA	Ptner 1

Software Used to Create Schedules

We have not found a completely suitable method of tracking due dates as part of tax preparation software, so we recommend separate tax control software. This has a disadvantage in that it is another database that needs to be maintained. This causes additional work entering the information and reconciling the two systems. However, when using the tax preparation software, it is also a separate step for you to enter the returns that need to be prepared when you know what has to be done. It is also necessary to enter the information as soon as you know what is to be prepared so you can track due dates for extensions and possibly estimated taxes. On the tax preparation system, marking it off when the return is completed is automatic or one click; on the separate system, however, it has to be entered and needs to be entered timely. The separate software, though, can handle multiple due dates for state returns, selected estimated tax due dates for clients that are not "protected" where separate calculations have to be made for each quarterly payment, and forms and filings and follow-up information where there is no actual tax form such as Crummey letters, officer loan interest payments, personal auto inclusion in W-2 amounts, and tax refund filings.

Some firms create Excel spreadsheets, while others use their billing programs.

How the Schedule Will Be Tracked

Many firms have a method whereby they prepare a new client checklist as they get new clients. That form lists the tax returns the firm is responsible for preparing. The form is usually saved in the client's permanent file. A problem arises when additional preparation work is to be done for an existing nontax preparation client. For instance, let's assume a client for whom you performed forensic litigation work now wants to become a regular client and have your firm prepare his or her tax returns. Well, this client has already been entered into your system with the new client checklist. There might not be any regular mechanism to now enter the tax returns you are asked to prepare during the next tax season. (You might have done a pre-year-end tax projection for him or her, but that would not ordinarily be entered onto the tax control.) We suggest that the new client checklist be renamed "New Service" checklist and that it be filled out immediately whenever a new service is known to be performed for a client. As a matter of good business practice, you can also list the fee and billing arrangement. These matters will then be fresh in your mind, and you'll be forced to resolve the issue at that time instead of leaving it open-ended or vague.

The tax calendar should be networked, with access to entering and updating data.

An added client service and practice support process is to prepare an individualized tax and financial payments calendar for a client. The starting point would be the tax calendar you maintain, but you would include estimated or actual expected payment amounts. Obviously, this would be prepared only when your client service arrangement includes this add-on premium service.

Setting Priorities

People who are not corporate clients usually have their returns assigned according to who is available. If at all possible, you should try to schedule the same person who prepared the client's return in the past.

Scheduling and preparing of returns should usually be done on a first in first out (FIFO) basis. Unless someone has a dire need for a tax return by a specific date, such as leaving the country or going on an extended vacation, you should not take returns out of the order that they came in.

Time Needed to Complete a Return

The amount of time it takes to get a return to the client for many firms is approximately 3 weeks before March 31 and 10 days or sooner from April 1 on.

After April 15, the process can take approximately one month because people are not necessarily scheduled to be in the office to do tax returns as they are during tax season. Tax returns are also not given the full priority after April 15 that they are usually given beforehand because of the lack of serious government deadlines. However, the faster you can get the return out, the more satisfied your client.

The more voluminous the returns, the longer the review and the higher the potential for error. Therefore, the preparation of difficult tax returns should be scheduled to minimize the strain and number of client telephone calls. For difficult returns, you should call the client and work out a time for him or her to submit his or her information, telling the client who will be working on his or her return and when it can be expected to be completed. You can also schedule a reviewer to specifically review that return and have the preparer and reviewer coordinate this with each other.

In general, we have a two week completed return policy. This policy greatly reduces client calls, reduces our work in process, eliminates most scheduling problems, and speeds up our cash flow. Not too bad!

Review Staff Arrangements and Responsibilities 8

Firms start tax season weekend work any time from the beginning of January to the beginning of February. This usually includes either Saturday or Sunday and night work two times per week. Some firms require night work on an as-needed basis. Very few public accounting firms do not have extra hours during tax season.

Some firms close the day after April 15, and some have a golf outing for partners.

Some firms restrict the night and weekend work solely to tax return preparation. No audit work can be done, except in some rare instances.

Some firms pay overtime weekly or with each paycheck; other firms accumulate overtime until a date after tax season but usually no later than June 30. Others do not specifically pay for tax season work but give a bonus, taking into account the added time and effort during tax season. Some do not pay anything extra, instead working the extra hours into the regular weekly pay arrangement.

Some firms that pay overtime base it on straight time over 40 hours per week, and some firms pay time and a half. State labor laws might determine how you should pay for overtime hours. Some firms have a 35- or 37½-hour work week but pay no overtime until 40 hours per week are exceeded.

For their staff working during tax season, some firms bring in lunch, others dinner, and some both. Some firms pay a fixed-dollar amount for dinner and let their staff make their own arrangements for eating.

Whatever the arrangement, firms need to focus on two items: accountability and control through an effective tracking system and using personnel to their full potential.

Accountability and Control

To ensure control and accountability, an effective time tracking system must be maintained on a real-time (that is, daily) basis.

Updating our daily time system eliminates any need for additional timesheets or recordkeeping. Some purposes and benefits of the daily entries are as follows:

- To know how much time was spent on a return and by whom. In many cases, returns are touched by people whom the partners are unaware.
- To track progress by looking at the accumulated time, rather than by speaking to, or calling, a staff person.
- To know who is currently handling the return.
- To track the work a staff person has done the previous day, especially a day he or she might not have been in the office. Another reason is that the system allows us to deal with situations such as seeing staff congregating around the office, wondering what they were doing and accomplishing, and being able to check their work the next morning when they choose to.
- To determine whether a staff person is working on scheduled work or impromptu, unscheduled, or unplanned work.
- To track that the proper time is charged to a job and to make sure that nonchargeable activities are not charged to a client for whom the staff did not perform work.
- To determine that a staff person is working adequate hours during periods of unusual extra work or that a staff person is working an inordinate amount of time.
- To make sure that all work that is done is captured in the time system while it is fresh in the minds of the accountants.
- To be able to bill when a return is sent to a client, not after one month or longer.

Using Personnel Effectively

For personnel to operate effectively during tax season, the firm has to recognize the human assets available and the relative scarcity of these resources. Briefly put, the resources, in order of ease of obtaining, are as follows:

- Administrative and support staff
- Preparers (usually lower-level staff)
- Reviewers (usually specialists or higher-level staff)
- Partners

The roles of each of these resources in the tax preparation process should be as follows.

Administrative and Support Staff

- Assemble and prepare the returns for sending to the client and filing with the tax authorities.
- Print the completed, ready-to-file return to your paperless filing system.
- Scan the client information and working papers into your system or into smart scanners
- Schedule appointments with clients.
- Inform mail-in clients that their information has been received.
- Log in client information as it arrives.
- Follow up to see that the clients have received their returns and that they send back the e-filing forms.
- Call the client for additional information when it is easily identifiable.
- Generally assist staff and partners to reduce their time in nonpreparation tasks.
- Assemble and turn around returns in one day.
- At the end of each day, enter returns and processing sheets into paperless filing system.

Preparers

- Prepare the returns.
- Do light research.
- Follow directions and attend to the details of preparing a return.
- Understand that what they do will be reviewed; they should prepare their work in a manner that makes it easy for the reviewer to review, and their work should be devoid of errors.
- Resolve questions and open items so that the reviewer doesn't have to do so.

- Call clients' questions and comments to the attention of their supervisor, manager, or partner. Make sure responses are generated when necessary or required.
- Organize the client's information in a specific order so the reviewer and partner can easily check the input if they choose. The organization should be done so the reviewer does not have to recreate what the preparer has done.
- Fill out standardized worksheets and schedules.
- Read and respond to checklist questions. Look up answers to questions that are not understood. Don't pass on them or indicate "N/A."
- Prepare self-checking worksheets.
- File memos, if any, and look at the final return to determine that it makes sense and meets expectations based on prior year activity and current year projections.
- The biggest return on investment is at the preparer level; therefore, it is essential that they are aware of the purpose of what they are doing; are properly trained; and follow firm procedures, checklists, and systems.
- The preparer should be aware of the impression he or she gives to the reviewer, and it should be one that the preparer is proud of, not cluttered with errors.

Reviewers

- Review returns.
- Be aware of different review methods: a content review that checks the input and an issues review with the purpose of saving the client taxes.
- Apply the methods of reviewing each return based on the preparer's skill level, the image of the preparer that the reviewer has developed (if any), the complexity of the return, and any easily apparent errors.
- Look for ways to prevent tax notices.
- Identify and eliminate or resolve red flags.
- Fully use the available tools, such as checklists, standardized worksheets, tax comparison schedules, and the ability to consult with firm specialists.

- The reviewer is the go-to person and tax consultant to the staff and should be fully familiar with all of the firm's resources.
- Provide continuous enforcement of compliance with established firm procedures and checklists.
- Teach the preparer by providing feedback so that there are no repetitive errors, which will also provide the chance for the preparer to self-train. Feedback must be timely.
- Understand that training and coaching is a continuous process that might need to be repeated numerous times with some staff members (which then may become a staff evaluation issue).
- Identify repeated or widespread errors, and develop forms or training to eliminate them.
- Reviewers should meet regularly during tax season to discuss issues that developed during their reviews. An easy method is weekly lunches. After tax season, monthly meetings can be held. If the firm has only one reviewer, then I suggest the meeting be with the partners—it doesn't need to be over lunch.
- The reviewer must be aware that when he or she approves a return with a preparer error, it becomes the reviewer's error, and he or she becomes fully responsible for that incorrect return. Proper care and attention must always be the reviewer's primary focus.

Because there are fewer reviewers than preparers, processes must be developed that will save the reviewers' time. These procedures might take extra time for the preparers, but their time is more readily available than the reviewers' and less expensive. Also, the better organized and prepared the return, the less time the reviewer will need to spend on the return.

Partners

- This category can also include senior managers, depending on the firm.
- Partners should delegate everything that can be delegated, including effectively delegating to each other when another partner can do something better.
- Partners should be available to answer questions about the client, resolve issues, and make sure no one is chasing their tail and the work is moving.

- An important role of the partner is to be able to discuss arising issues with the client and to make the client aware of any problems, bottlenecks, and the need for additional services.
- The partner has to be able to manage his or her book of business or client responsibilities a little better than during the rest of the year because staff won't be as available as they are during nontax season time.
- The partner has to let the clients know that the firm is open for business during tax season, not just open for tax return preparation.
- The partner is ultimately responsible for the proper functioning of tax season, the flow of work, and the accuracy and planning done for clients. The tax return is a reflection of that responsibility. It is incumbent upon the partners to ensure that proper training and systems are in place.

Effectively Using Your Main Resource

Accounting firms have many resources whose use has to be scheduled, coordinated, and monitored. Hard assets, such as the office and its environment, are one resource. A second resource is technology (covered in chapter 3), and a third resource is personnel or human resources. For accounting firms personnel is the most valuable resource.

A measure of effective staff utilization is realization. *Realization* is the fees collected divided by the time charges. Anything greater than 1 is fantastic. Most will agree that a realization of 85 percent or better is acceptable. Between 85 percent and 70 percent is a danger area. Lower than 70 percent is usually unacceptable.

When reviewing the realization percentage, allowances should be made for staff training time, learning a new specialty, excessive overhead charges included in the time run, and unanticipated extras.

Tax season realization is important because many of the tax returns are done for once-a-year clients, with added staff overtime and other costs that should be recoverable with proper billing. Another part of tax season is the preparation of individual returns for business and organization clients in which the bulk of the revenues are from the organization billing, not the tax returns. However, overtime and other costs still exist for this work.

Part of tax season and tax preparation work is the corporate, partnership, and not-for-profit returns that are also done during this period. Many firms have highly qualified managers and staff work on the financial statements for these clients and then assign the tax return preparation to a lower-level person who is unfamiliar with the client. The return is then given to a tax reviewer without the manager of that client overseeing the preparation or even looking at the return. This can lead to a lower quality product that is then over reviewed by a reviewer who can get worn out by checking detail work rather than issues. Here is a suggestion:

(1) the return should be prepared by a member of the financial statement engagement team,

(2) another member of the team should make sure the numbers tie in, and

(3) the manager on the account should do a top side review (look over the return to see if there are any missed issues) before it is turned in for review.

Scheduling should be done so that there are a minimum number of touches of the file. Don't schedule a two day return to someone who will only be in the office one day per week. For large returns, the reviewer should be scheduled in advance, with the preparer and reviewer coordinating the schedule.

Maximizing Tax Season Efficiency 9

Run your tax season as if you were advising a client on his or her business.

- Schedule the flow of work
  - Client meetings.
  - Client submission of data.
  - Based on staff availability.
- Schedule the proper level of staff to prepare the return
  - Availability of mentors or trainers.
  - Availability of proper tools and instructions on how the staff should use them.
- Schedule reviewers for big, complicated, or difficult returns
  - Assign returns to the proper level of reviewer.
- Reduce touches
  - Eliminate the reasons for excessive touches.
    - Don't start a return until all the information is in the office (except possibly for K-1s).
    - Organize follow-up procedures for missing information.
    - Have staff available to complete returns they started.
- Time systems track touches—look at the systems timely
- Examine extension procedures and consider reducing extensions
  - Who prepares extensions and when?
  - How are extensions delivered to the client?
  - Consider preparing extensions in late January or early February for clients who typically go on extension—get them done before your busy season gets started
- Prepare estimated taxes vouchers for the four quarters when extensions are prepared
  - If not, do you have a mini tax season for June 15th estimated tax vouchers?
  - If possible, include the first quarterly estimate with the balance due with the extension.

- Examine bottlenecks
  - Are pressure points at the reviewers' or assemblers' desks?
  - Most firms don't have pressure with preparers being backed up; rather, the pressure is waiting for the reviewer to get to the return.
  - A backlog may be created because of unanswered questions for many returns that are almost or as much as 90 percent completed.
- What is the relationship between the time the return is prepared versus the time spent reviewing the return?
  - What is the relationship between the time the return is prepared versus the time spent quality controlling the return?
  - Does using the term "quality control" rather than a review change your take on this process?
- Tax returns in process are your inventory. What do you tell clients about their inventory size?
- Accounts receivable and work in process (uncompleted tax returns, which also could be referred to as *inventory in process*) are wasting assets; the longer you have them, the less they are worth.
- Try to measure productivity (define this word any way you want) per preparer. My guess is that the slower, more deliberate preparers will have greater productivity because they didn't have to redo every return they worked on and because they cause less work for the reviewers and partners. Comment: Many partners do not look at overall productivity for slower workers concentrating on their slowness rather that the benefits of their careful work as it affects the reviewer, redos, and the quality of the returns the partners get to sign. Productivity is a measure of results, not time spent. In the aggregate, the better staff will have an overall higher realization, assuming fees are uniformly billed, because the clients they worked on will have had fewer touches on their work. Caution: in some firms, the better staff are put on the "better" clients, i.e. those with higher fees. In some regard, higher fee clients could have lower realization because the fees are not what they should be for all the services provided to the client. So you use better staff and earn less money. The flip side is that less skilled staff get put on smaller or not as desirable clients, and somehow, realization ends up better on those clients because of less supervision and, possibly, less uncompensated extra work.

- Use technology to its fullest extent. Effective technology can reduce dependence on additional staff.
- Look at the way you bring in lunch and dinners to determine whether it increases or decreases efficiency.
- Be clear about what needs to be done for each client and make sure your staff are also clear. If a client told you that he or she does not want to pay you extra for entering his or her checks into QuickBooks and the client sends you his or her checks unsorted, what do you do about it? Is your staff on the same page as you? What about the staff person who also prepares a bank reconciliation and corrects extensive errors because of that? The staff should be aware of what the engagement is to cover and what needs to be done.
- Your staff should have neat, uncluttered desks and work areas.

SECTION II

Return Preparation—Overview and Introduction to Tax Comparison Worksheets 10

Tax season and preparation has provided many firms with the impetus to introduce new ideas and improve the firm. Clients are filling out their organizers online and receiving their returns by e-mail. With the accounting firm filing the returns electronically, not a single piece of paper is generated.

The issue is to recognize that there is a system and that the procedures must be followed to ensure a smooth, or smoother, tax season. The steps in this system include the following:

- The client calls for an appointment and speaks to either the administrative assistant or a partner (chapter 11).
- Clients needing tax interviews meet with a partner; others send in their information via mail or e-mail (chapter 11).
- Client information is copied or scanned and organized. Client active status is recorded into the tax control (chapter 11).
- The return is prepared by an accountant (not necessarily the person who conducted the interview). Some issues may need to be researched, and this may be done by someone else (chapter 12).
- The return is reviewed and could be given back to the preparer if there is a question or for a change to be made (chapter 13).
- Time charges are calculated or a fixed fee schedule is filled out, and the bill is prepared. Bills are distributed to the bookkeeper (chapter 14).
- A partner approves the issuance of the return. The return is copied and assembled, or a digital copy is e-mailed to client. Paper versions of returns, or copies, are mailed by an administrative assistant (chapter 14).

- Appropriate returns are e-filed (chapter 15).
- Extensions are prepared. The process starts over regarding obtaining information from clients with extensions (chapter 16).
- A client calls with tax audit notices (chapter 17).
- Checks are received from clients with completed returns, and we use the money to spend on a vacation to recover from tax season.
- The last extension is filed on October 15. Tomorrow, tax season starts again.

There is a system, and it works.

Excel Tax Comparison Worksheets as a Review, Training, Planning, and User-Friendly Tool

It is not often that a single tool serves multiple highly essential purposes. The Excel tax comparison worksheet[1] we developed is such a tool.

The worksheet is a simple comparison of the client's current and previous years' tax returns, with some variations that make it easier to review returns, train staff, plan with the client, and give the client a user-friendly summary of his or her tax return that promotes better meetings and discussions. Please note that the worksheets are not a calculation method but a means of presentation.

Almost every tax preparation program produces tax comparison schedules with the prior year. The problem with these programs is that they cover the categories and totals as they appear on the tax return, not as the client understands his or her income, expenses, and tax situation. The Excel tax comparison worksheets correct these deficiencies.

The Tool Described

The Excel worksheet has columns for the current year and last few years. The line items from the tax return are entered on the worksheet, with the exception of K-1 components, which are grouped together. Additionally, an extra column is usually included for a projection of the current year.

---

[1] Any spreadsheet program can be used. We use Excel and describe the tool as such, but it is not an Excel product. Excel is a trademark of Microsoft Corporation.

Occasionally, we also include the column of the projection for the previous year for which the return has just been completed, so a comparison can be made of how close the final return came to the projection. The comparison columns also provide a frame of reference and isolate large differences between the projection and actual return amounts or between the previous and current years.

The K-1 items are grouped to more meaningfully present the client's income. For example, a K-1 with high interest income that is not so grouped would be included with the interest income as it appeared on the tax return and would distort the client's actual personal interest income when he or she was looking at or analyzing his or her income for the year. On the other hand, not including it with the other K-1 activities would distort the net income or loss from the entity providing the K-1. Clients usually never think of the individual parts of the K-1s; they only know the net result.

This matter can be illustrated by the example of a client getting a K-1 with $50,000 interest income and a $40,000 business operating loss. The actual income or loss from the entity was $10,000. That is the way the client will relate to that entity. The client could also have $5,000 interest income from bonds and savings accounts. However, the tax return will show $55,000 as interest income (which the client usually won't be able to easily relate to) and a $40,000 operating loss (which he or she also won't easily be able to relate to). The Excel worksheet would show $5,000 interest income and $10,000 income from the entity. Using the Excel worksheets makes it easier for the client to understand his or her financial situation and plan and for us to advise the client. It also makes comparing the client's activities and return easier.

When applicable, additional Excel schedules can be prepared to provide summaries of the client's interest and dividend income by account or payer, with a distribution analysis of taxability by the federal government and each state where the client is subject to tax. You can also prepare summaries of rental property and Schedule Cs.

The Excel file can additionally have a worksheet providing an analysis of tax carryforwards, including Schedule E rental property items, capital gains, business operating losses, investment interest expense, charity deductions, and alternative minimum tax credit availability.

For clients with simple returns for whom you don't do projections, or who are without K-1s, multiple accounts, property or Schedule Cs, you can use the two-year comparison from your tax preparation software. The Excel worksheet is a tool and should be incorporated into your overall tax preparation process.

Using the Excel Worksheets in the Review Process

The Excel worksheet is an effective review tool. The actual numbers on the final return are entered on the Excel worksheet and compared with the projection for that year, if one was done, and the previous year's actual amounts. The reviewer will also eyeball the actual amounts from the prior two or three years. Comparing each item can be easily done in a matter of 1–2 minutes or 5–10 minutes for involved returns. Any major variances can easily be identified and then researched in the client's documents. Using this method will identify almost every major, material, illogical, or unexpected difference. When I am supervising a preparer, I review the Excel worksheet (not the return) for differences and accuracy of the preparation prior to having the preparer hand in the return for the actual review.

Because the preparer is aware of the review procedure with the worksheet, the preparer would be best advised to perform these steps before handing in the return for review. It is always better for the preparer, rather than the reviewer, to find the errors.

This prereview process by the preparer also allows him or her to take a few moments to look at the big picture and reflect on what he or she did. It is amazing how many of their own errors the preparers find.

Using the Excel worksheets also makes it easier to look for and uncover tax or financial planning possibilities for the client. Even if it is too late for planning for the return that was just prepared, or the year that just ended, planning can be recommended for the current year or later years. When doing the prereview of the return by comparing and possibly reconciling it with the projection, don't overlook the opportunity to save the client tax dollars by recommending he or she apply for refunds for the previous two years.

Using the Excel Worksheets for Training

We cannot overemphasize the need for thorough, directed training of preparers and reviewers. The importance of training the preparers is to get a better product that will be easier to review and, therefore, free up the reviewer's mind to look for tax saving opportunities instead of spending most of his or her time ticking and tying.

The Excel worksheet is an effective tool that can train the preparer. We said earlier that the preparer should use the Excel worksheet to compare the completed return with the projection and last year's return and make sure there are no great differences. By completing the Excel worksheet, the preparer is virtually forced to make this comparison. If he or she does not, it will become obvious to the reviewer and will necessitate him or her finding out why the preparer entered numbers on the worksheet without thinking. "Knock knock—is anyone there?"

Any large differences between the items for prior years and the current year should be looked into to make sure no errors were made. When projections were done, the comparison should also be made with the projection. All of this should be explained to the preparer.

Another training tip: many preparers might do a diligent job of preparing the return and tying in all their work, but they neglect to look at the final return that they just completed. Experienced reviewers easily uncover many errors by simply looking at the output and comparing it with the previous year's return. Such errors can include incorrect Social Security numbers, addresses, and spelling of clients' names. Getting the preparer to do this first would raise the quality of the finished product passed on to the reviewer and reduce the reviewer's time, the error correction time, and the total processing and handling time. This is not instead of the Excel worksheets but in addition to them.

Planning

The planning part of the Excel worksheet is better done when the essential information is presented in an easy-to-digest bird's eye view. This eliminates time and effort shuffling papers. Even though a projection might be prepared using dedicated projection software or the tax projection feature of your preparation program, the information should also be entered on the Excel worksheet. In many cases, the over 20 pages of output, including summary sheets, do not show the data in an easy-to-view manner. Therefore, the summaries should be entered on an Excel worksheet. The better the presentation of the information, the more effective and substantive the meeting.

We also prepare extensive Excel worksheets for basis and suspended loss calculations, nonstatutory options, and incentive stock options. For some clients, we track cash flow information reported on the K-1 schedules.

Cross-Selling Opportunities

Almost every tax client needs additional services the preparer can provide. The issue becomes not how to approach the client with suggestions but when. Not doing so eliminates an opportunity to better serve the client and improve your revenue and client relationship.

One way is to keep a follow-up list of advice that you've given to the client at your projection or tax information meetings. Another way is to scan your meeting notes and put them in a folder that you can review after tax season. Yet another method is to collect copies of the Excel tax return summaries that a partner then reviews to determine if there are additional tax or financial planning opportunities for the client. You can also specifically review all clients with a Schedule C to see if a pension plan is applicable and, if so, call them. Finally, you can suggest opening a Keogh plan, a simplified employee pension (SEP) plan, a SIMPLE IRA, or defined benefit plans or to exercise stock options and triggers in deferred compensation plans, when appropriate.

Notice to Skeptics

I have found that most people are reluctant to try the Excel worksheets because

- it is a new method (not to me because I have been using them for over 30 years).
- it adds time (only at the lower levels. It is not good business management to save the time of the lowest levels at the expense of the higher levels or to not try to save the time of the most valuable personnel who cost more and are in much shorter supply).
- the staff will resist it with every morsel of strength they have. The staff are the ones not producing high quality work that they have

neglected to self-reviewed beforehand. If they did excellent work, their pride in their work would make them willing to try new things.
- the partners need to oversee the implementation of the program and cannot permit exceptions. I have found that when training, allowing exceptions effectively destroys the system you are trying to introduce.
- if you were a manufacturer, the cost of a machine and its installation and training would be measured against the future benefits. Do that with this program. It works. Trust me on that.

A last word to skeptics: have one person try the Excel worksheets on the next three returns he or she works on and then evaluate the overall effectiveness. Also, if you e-mail me at emendlowitz@withum.com, I will email you back a pro forma Excel file to help get you started. I'll also give you my cell phone number, so you can call me with any questions. And if you tried the three returns and have questions, do not hesitate to contact me and I will be glad to review your process with you.

Sample Excel Worksheets

Following are five sample Excel tax comparison and projection worksheets.

The first worksheet is the basic worksheet that is prepared for everyone, regardless of whether we do a projection. The first page has a summary of the last few years and a column for the current year's projection. If a projection is not being done for that client, or at that time, this column is omitted. We include this worksheet with the actual final tax return as a multiyear summary. The second page has a summary of the taxes due and tax payments.

The second worksheet has a summary of the client's K-1 schedules. The totals from this worksheet are transferred to the basic worksheet. What the client will see is a summary of all his or her K-1s and what he or she is taxed on.

The third schedule shows the details of all the 1099s for interest and dividends. Again, the totals are shown on the basic worksheet to indicate the client's total interest and dividend activity for the year.

The fourth and fifth Excel comparison worksheets are prepared for rental properties and schedule C items, as appropriate for the client.

Sample Excel Tax Comparison and Projection Worksheet

George and Martha Washington
Client #
Tax Comparison
Prepared: 10/11/XX SP

Status: Married Filing Joint	**200P Actual**	**200Q Actual**	**200R Actual**	**200S Actual**	**20TT Projection**	**Comments**
Wages						
Alpha Company	104,000	110,000	112,000	–		
Beta Company	22,500	21,000	30,000	32,000		
Interest Income (not K-1)	16,436	5,867	6,420	5,801		
Less: Tax-exempt Interest	(8,389)	(918)	(929)	(1,022)		
Dividend Income	1,561	2,210	2,043	2,012		
State Tax Refund				1,200		
Less: nontaxable due to tax benefit rule						
Capital Gains (Losses)						
Current Year (not K-1)	(9,566)	(105,715)	20,903	6,345		
Current Year (Vacation House sale)				101,000		
Current Year (Vacation Condo)				88,000		
Non-Business Bad Debt – Alpha Company				(68,000)		
Cap Gain Distributions	99					
C/O from prior yr	(19,000)	(25,467)	(128,182)	(104,279)		
C/O to next year	25,467	128,182	104,279			
IRA Distributions		200,000		159		
Less: rollover		(200,000)				

K-1s:						
Ordinary Income (Loss)	(6,270)	(7,210)	(5,270)	1,149		
Rental Real Estate Income (Loss)	(7,676)	(9,411)	(8,812)	(8,618)		
Other Income (Loss)						
K-1 Interest Income	2,818	8,346	(3,100)	17,234		
Social Security Benefits	16,320	16,544	16,891	17,354		
Less: Non-taxable amount	(2,448)	(2,482)	(2,534)	(2,603)		
Other Income (Loss):						
Atlantic & Pacific, P.A.				25,000		
Adjustments to Income:						
Penalty on Early W/D of savings (K-1)				(2,371)		
1/2 Self-employment tax	(377)			(361)		
Adjusted Gross Income	135,475	140,946	143,709	110,000		
Itemized Deductions:						
Medical						
State Income Taxes						
Estimated Tax & Extension Payments	500		1,667			
State & Local Taxes	31	31	–	3,258		
Real Estate Tax	12,478	14,926	16,665	18,646		
Mortgage Interest	14,410	13,430	13,114	12,545		
Charitable Contributions:						
Current year cash	2,913	1,925	1,928	1,817		
Current year non-cash				9,420		

(continued)

	200P Actual	200Q Actual	200R Actual	200S Actual	20TT Projection	Comments
3% Limitation						
Total Itemized Deductions	30,332	30,312	33,374	45,686		
Exemptions	6,000	6,100	6,300	6,400		
Taxable Income	99,143	104,534	104,035	57,914		
Federal Tax:						
Federal Tax	9,448	8,791	12,670	3,833		
Foreign Tax Credit			(107)	–		
Household Employment Tax						
Self-employment Tax				721		
Total Federal Tax	9,448	8,791	12,563	4,554		
State Taxes:	1,890	1,758	2,513	911		
Total Federal & State Tax Liability	11,338	10,549	15,076	5,465		

Sample Excel Tax Comparison and Projection Worksheet

Schedule of Payments & Tax Due	**Federal**	**Federal**	**Federal**	**Federal**		
Federal Tax Per Above	**9,448**	**8,791**	**12,563**	**4,554**		
Overpayment from Prior Year		324	2,927	2,431		
Federal Income Tax Withheld	3,412	3,318	3,701	(2,120)		
Est. Pmt. 4/15	4,500	2,100	–	–		
Est. Pmt. 6/15		2,100	–	–		
Est. Pmt. 9/15		2,100	4,093	–		
Est. Pmt. 1/15		2,100	2,200			
Amount Paid with Extension			5,000	6,000		
Excess Social Security Tax Withheld	1,860					
Total Payments	9,772	11,718	14,994	3,880		
Federal Amount You Owe (Overpaid)	(324)	(2,927)	(2,431)	674		
Estimated Tax Penalty		–		46		
Late Payment		–				
Interest		–				
Federal Amount Owed (Overpaid) 4/15	**1,805**	**(2,532)**	**(2,431)**	**720**		
	State	**State**	**State**	**State**	**State**	
State Tax Per Above	–	–	–	–		
State Tax Withheld				–		
Estimated Pmt by 12/31						

(continued)

Schedule of Payments & Tax Due	**Federal**	**Federal**	**Federal**	**Federal**		
Federal Tax Per Above	**9,448**	**8,791**	**12,563**	**4,554**		
State Extension payment						
State Amount You Owe (Overpaid)	–	–	–	–		

Sample Excel Tax Comparison and Projection Worksheet
K-1 Summary Schedule

John and Abigail Adams
Tax summary worksheet
Tax year 20YY
Prepared Nov 4, 20YY

K-1 and Grantor Trust Summary

Entity	W/P Ref	P/A	ST	**20YY Proj**	**20XX** Net Effect of K-1's	Income (Loss)	Rental Income	Interest Income	Long-Term Sec. 1231	Capital Gain/(Loss)	179 Deduction	Charity	Penalty on early draw
Associates	11A	P	NY		26,035		24,963	1,072					2,371
Group (Final in 2002)		P	NY		–								
S S Corp (John)	11J	A	NY		(35,887)	(38,065)		2,178					
S S Corp (Abigail)	11K	A	NY		(362)	(384)		22					
Alpha Company		A	NY		(136,192)	25,691			(1,613)	(137,317)	(22,953)	(2,799)	
US 1 Realty		P	NY		10		10						
Private Realty, LLC	11B	P	MD		(7,061)		(7,061)						
Semi Private Realty, LLC		P	MD		(47)	(47)							
Public Investments LLC (John)			PA		(51,157)	(51,181)		24					
Public Investments LLC (Abigail)			PA		(517)	(517)		–					

(continued)

Entity	W/P Ref	P/A	ST	20YY Proj	20XX Net Effect of K-1's	Income (Loss)	Rental Income	Interest Income	Long-Term Sec. 1231	Capital Gain/(Loss)	179 Deduction	Charity	Penalty on early draw
Comfortable Apartment Group	11E	P	DC		11,854	11,804		50					
Uncomfy You Bet LLC	11L	P	DC		287,465		(10,090)	720	296,835				
BTO Realty	11G	P	DC		82,846		82,836	10					
Total Partnership K-1's					**176,987**	**(52,699)**	**90,658**	**4,076**	**295,222**	**(137,317)**	**(22,953)**	**(2,799)**	**2,371**
Gamma Company	11M	A	MS		599,999	(158,760)		2,068	756,691			(180)	
Total S-Corp K-1's					**599,999**	**(158,760)**	**–**	**2,068**	**756,691**	**–**	**–**	**(180)**	
Total Grantor Trust Income					**120,000**	**–**	**120,000**	**–**	**–**	**–**		**–**	
Total K-1 and Grantor Trust Income					**896,986**	**(211,459)**	**210,658**	**6,144**	**1,051,913**	**(137,317)**	**(22,953)**	**(2,979)**	**2,371**
						↘	(22,953)	179 expense		line 12 of Sch D			line 30 of 1040
Ordinary K-1 Income							(211,459)						
1231 Gain							–						
Prior Disallowed Passive Losses													
Prior Disall. Pub Tr Ptsp Passive Losses							–						
Disallowed Passive Losses							–		–				
Disallowed Pub Tr Ptship Passive Losses							–		Sch D line 11				
Pass Through Income (Loss)							(23,754)		1,051,913				
							Form 1040, Line 17		**Form 1040, Line 14**				

Sample Excel Tax Comparison and Projection Worksheet

Interest and Dividend Supporting Schedules

Thomas and Roberta Jefferson
Tax worksheet summary
Tax year 20XX
Prepared Nov 4, 20XX

SCHEDULE 1 – INTEREST INCOME			**20XX Proj**	**20WW**	**FEDERAL**				
		W/P		**Total**		**Muni-Tax**	**US**	**Inv.**	**AMT**
Payer of Interest	**Account #**	**Ref**		**Received**	**Interest**	**Exempt**	**Obligation**	**Int. pd**	**Adj.**
JP Morgan – Thomas				1,357	1,357				
JP Morgan – Joint				2,529	2,529				
North Fork Bank				326	326				
UBS Fin/PaineWebber				18,371	18,371				
UBS Fin Services				2,374	2,374				
1600 Penn Ave Loan				13,067	13,067				
Capital One – CD				3,355	3,355				
Merrill Lynch – George				6	6				
Fidelity				1,547		1,547			
ING Direct – Thomas				5,668	5,668				
ING Direct – Roberta				25	25				
Sub-total				**48,625**	**47,078**	**1,547**	–	–	–
From K-1					56,030				
Reclass, US obligation									
Tax Exempt Dividends									
Total Interest				**48,625**	**103,108**	**1,547**			

(continued)

SCHEDULE 2 – DIVIDEND INCOME			20XX Proj	20WW	FEDERAL				
		W/P		Total	Ord	Cap Gn	Tax	Foreign	AMT
Payer of Dividend	Account #	Ref		Received	Div	Dist	Exempt	Tax Paid	Adj.
Fidelity				891	–		891		501
Ameritrade				–	–				
Salomon Smith Barney				–	–				
Salomon Smith Barney				–	–				
Merrill Lynch				1,430	1,430				
Ryan Beck & Co.				–	–				
UBS Fin Services				–	–				
UBS Fin Services				–	–				
Capital One				–	–				
Phoenix Companies				–	–				
Phoenix Companies				–	–				
Phoenix Companies				–	–				
Sub-total				**2,321**	**1,430**	**–**	**891**	**–**	**501**
From K-1 and Grantor Trust									
Totals									

Sample Excel Tax Comparison and Projection Worksheet
Schedule C Supporting Schedule

John and Abigail Adams
Tax summary worksheet
Tax year 20YY
Prepared Apr 4, 20YY

Schedule C
John's Consulting Business

	20UU	20VV	20WW	20XX
Revenues	**176,002**	**201,090**	**223,087**	**268,034**
Cost of sales	14,316	16,357	18,146	21,802
Gross profit	**161,686**	**184,733**	**204,941**	**246,232**
Advertising	2,800	2,800	3,200	3,600
Auto expenses	2,315	2,945	3,120	2,980
Commissions	12,000	12,000	12,000	16,000
Depreciation	0	0	4,235	0
Insurance	3,340	3,641	3,968	4,325
Legal and professional services	6,000	6,480	7,200	7,776
Office expenses	1,300	1,400	1,700	1,860
Rent	12,000	12,600	13,230	13,892

(continued)

	20UU	20VV	20WW	20XX
Auto lease	4,140	4,140	4,140	4,920
Repairs and maintenance	378	401	425	450
Supplies	426	452	479	507
Licenses	120		120	
Travel	12,099	13,672	15,449	17,458
Meals	10,645	12,029	13,593	15,360
Less nondeductible meals	5,323	6,014	6,796	7,680
Utilities	1,209	1,344	1,495	1,662
Other expenses				
Fed Ex and Courier	2,409	2,843	3,354	3,958
Conventions	13,901	16,403	19,356	22,840
Website maintenance	3,600	4,248	5,013	5,915
Outside services	6,000	7,080	8,354	9,858
Total expenses	**100,005**	**110,491**	**127,227**	**141,041**
Net income	**61,681**	**74,242**	**77,714**	**105,191**

Sample Excel Tax Comparison and Projection Worksheet
Schedule E Supporting Schedule

John and Abigail Adams
Tax summary worksheet
Tax year 20YY
Prepared Apr 4, 20YY

Schedule E
Rental property – 246 88th Street, Your City, NJ

	20UU	20VV	20WW	20XX
Rent income	**112,000**	**118,720**	**96,001**	**133,009**
Advertising			3,400	
Cleaning and maintenance	3,360	3,461	3,565	3,672
Commissions			14,200	
Insurance	9,200	9,936	10,731	11,589
Legal and professional fees	800	800	3,100	800
Mortgage interest	39,890	38,494	37,147	35,846
Repairs	1,200	1,600	18,800	2,300
Supplies	346	362	378	395
Taxes	14,800	15,466	16,162	16,889
Utilities	4,480	4,682	4,892	5,112
Other				
Inspection fees	0	0	1,200	0
Snow removal	2,400	2,400	2,400	2,400

(continued)

	20UU	20VV	20WW	20XX
Depreciation	19,880	19,880	19,880	19,800
Total expenses	**96,356**	**97,080**	**135,854**	**98,884**
Net income	**15,644**	**21,640**	**–39,853**	**34,125**

Make Appointments with Clients 11

Each partner schedules his or her own appointments to interview clients. New clients are almost always seen by a partner. For larger practices or those with extensive once-a-year tax clients, an administrative person can schedule the appointments.

Making appointments is a pain in the neck, but essential. I set aside days, and some nights, to see tax clients. I schedule an hour per person, with some slack time to allow for running late or to return phone calls or e-mails. In a typical day, the first appointment might be at 9:30 A.M.; the second at 11:00 A.M.; the third at noon; the fourth at 1:30 P.M.; and then again at 3:00 P.M., 4:00 P.M., and possibly 5:00 P.M. or later for those who want to come after work. This schedule gives me potential to see six or seven people in one day. My administrative assistant or an office assistant calls clients who I typically see to schedule the appointments. I usually see people in different locations: my offices in New Brunswick and New York City and conference facilities in several parts of Manhattan and Long Island.

All audit people are to get information from the principals of our corporate clients sometime in February. If they do not, a continuous flow of calls must be made every third day until the information comes in. This might seem to be an annoyance to the client, and it is. However, the annoyance is offset by the rise in confidence in the firm knowing that someone is watching the return and won't let it slip through the cracks. In my mind, the extra telephone calls are a marketing maneuver.

When we make an appointment with a new client, we make sure to discuss our fees and the basis for them. For lower income clients, we give them a rate schedule. For wealthier clients, we prepare an engagement letter with a fee range. We also state when we expect to be paid, and we accept major credit cards. Note that many firms prepare engagement letters for all individual tax clients.

Receive Information From Clients

Information can be received from clients in two ways: a personal interview or mail. This section covers these two topics and engagement letters.

Tax Return Interview

Following are some procedures that could be followed when interviewing clients to get their income tax information:

- When you interview clients in person, ask them to bring all of the previous year's canceled checks or a printout if it's available. If they bring checks, ask the clients to sort them beforehand, or if they would prefer, you can perform data entry and give them an analysis of their entire year's expenditures.
- Record clients' home and business phone numbers on the control sheet.
- Ask all clients their birth date and record it in the working papers and on the tax input sheets.
- Ask all clients their children's ages. Social Security numbers are mandatory for all dependents. If clients do not have a Social Security number for a dependent, give clients Form SS-5.
- Verify if the client is an active participant in an employer-maintained retirement plan and whether the employer actually made a contribution for the client. If the employer did not make a contribution, the client might be able to make a deductible contribution to an IRA.
- When we get a new client, we try to obtain a copy of the previous year's tax return before we start our work.

Mail-In Clients

A number of clients mail us their information. Mail-in clients must be treated a little differently because you don't have personal eye-to-eye contact with them. We call the client to tell him or her that the information has arrived, who will work on the return, and approximately how long it will take until the return will be completed. Some mail-in clients have their returns scheduled, with the client being told when to mail us his or her information. Receiving the information too early will increase the flow of calls asking when the return will be ready.

Copies of any correspondence sent with the information are given to a partner, who will follow up with a telephone call if necessary.

You can also have an administrative person call a couple of days after the completed return has been sent to the client to make sure he or she received it and to inquire if there are any questions. Part of servicing mail-in clients should include creating or strengthening the bond between the client and firm.

Handling mail-in clients is similar to handling a direct marketing operation. As such, it might be propitious to take a course in direct marketing or read a book or series of articles. You are not using the direct marketing to get new business, but you are doing the fulfillment part, which is receiving the returns and sending them to the clients. That is the area you should concentrate on.

We correspond with clients by calling and sending e-mails to them to address their specific situations. For example, if we give a speech on asset allocation techniques, we send a client with those expressed concerns or needs a copy of the handout with a handwritten note to call us if he or she wants to discuss the issues further.

Engagement Letters

It is good business procedure to obtain an engagement letter for every client you prepare a return for. This has become an especially important tool to eliminate misunderstandings with the client and, perhaps, the clients' family members when there is intrafamily controversy.

A sample engagement letter is included in exhibit 11-1, "Sample Engagement Letter."

EXHIBIT 11-1 Sample Engagement Letter

[Date]

[Client Name]
[Client Address]

Dear [Client Name]:

As is customary in the profession, we are providing you with this engagement letter outlining the services this firm will render and the fee arrangements in connection with the preparation of your 20XX tax returns.

We will prepare your federal, state, and local income tax returns from information that you will furnish. We will not audit or otherwise verify the data you submit, although we may ask you to clarify portions of it. We will resolve questions involving the application of tax rules in your favor if there is reasonable justification.

The IRS, as well as state and local taxing authorities, reserve the right to examine your tax returns. The selection of tax returns for examination is usually based upon variances from standard norms. In many cases, however, selections are made on a random basis. Also, as your income increases, your chances for selection increase. Should your return be selected for examination at a later date, we will be available to represent you, and the time spent will be billed to you at our standard rates for tax examinations.

Our fees are based on the amount of time required to obtain, review, and analyze your information; perform any necessary research; and prepare and process your tax returns. My hourly rate through December 31, 20YY, will be $XXX. The hourly rate for other members of our firm will range from $XX to $XXX. In addition, you will be charged for out-of-pocket expenses (for example, messenger charges and computer service charges). Generally, you will be billed after we have completed your tax returns. Our invoices are due and payable immediately upon receipt. There will be a late charge equal to 1.5 percent per month on any unpaid balances.

If the preceding terms are in agreement with your understanding of our engagement, please sign and return the enclosed copy of this letter along with your organizer. Should you have any questions concerning this letter or the fees to be charged, please do not hesitate to call.

Thank you very much.

Very truly yours,

[***Partner Signature***]

Approved by: ______________________ __________

Signature *Date*

This letter was prepared by E. Martin Davidoff, CPA, Esq. Printed with permission.

Organize the Information and the File

Many offices are becoming paperless. However, before you can have a paperless system, you need a method of capturing and organizing the information. The following presents working paper and filing processes that were done manually and can be adapted to the paperless environment.

Whenever tax information comes in, the administrative assistant records it into the tax control program and copies or scans all the information that the preparer will need. If there are canceled checks for Schedule Cs, he or she enters them into QuickBooks. We do not keep any original information. All information to be returned is put in a separate envelope and kept with the file. It is returned when we send the client his or her return. The copies are put in the current year's file (either physically or saved on the client's file on the server), which is accompanied by the previous year's tax file (if not paperless) and a folder for next year. The files and client information are then put in the special filing cabinets where all in-process tax returns are kept.

All files in process must be put in specially designated filing cabinets. Doing so enables other staff personnel to quickly locate a file and complete a return. It also reduces clutter in the office and on individual desks. For firms with a paperless system, everything is always trackable and available to be retrieved from the cloud-based system. The original client-supplied documents should be scanned into the system and kept separate until it will be returned when the return is completed.

Nonpaperless Filing Procedures

At some point this will be the exception because most people I talk to are migrating to the Cloud. Nevertheless, until then, here are procedures you can follow.

I suggest you keep only the folders from the last two years in your office. At the same time, new file folders should be set up and made ready for the coming tax season. You should also keep file folders for the next year. In 2015, you would be preparing the 2014 tax returns, and will retain the 2012 and 2013 return folders and we have the 2015 file folders set up. All prior years should be kept in your storage area.

Separate filing cabinets can be maintained for individual tax returns, including gift, estate, and trust tax returns, and personal financial statement working papers and file folders; and a separate set of cabinets for business and organization files and "mint" copies of financial statements. Note that when this was written, I had just come from the new offices of a colleague and he had the administration area covered with wall-to-wall filing cabinets that reached to the ceiling. Using paperless procedures, he would have space for three additional people to work and eliminate the physical handling of the files—some of which are touched many times during tax season.

Individual, gift, estate, and trust files are filed by the client's last name. Corporate, partnership, and organization files are filed by the first letter of the first name of the entity. For example, if the corporate name is a person's name followed by *Inc.* or *P.C.*, the files will be in alphabetical order based on the first letter of that client's first name.

Files might include the following:

- *Tax file.* Use a separate file folder for each year. You can use manila folders with year tabs on the upper right edge. The tax file is set up so that a copy of the tax return and supporting working papers are filed on the right side. Every working paper must be fully indexed and cross-referenced, if necessary. Uniform working papers must be used, when applicable. The tax control is the top sheet. On the left side, are tax projections, analytical printouts from tax preparation software, tax research notes, copies of tax correspondence, and notices and pink flag sheets, if necessary.
- *Special matters.* When you work on a special matter for an individual client, you can use separate yellow file folders for each matter. This could be for divorce consulting, financial or estate planning, assistance in employment or other negotiations, IRA-required minimum distributions, or buying a business. Each matter has the year typed on the folder. Some folders could be for a process that runs over a few years, such as a marital separation. These are not removed from the filing cabinets for many years.
- *Permanent file.* When necessary, maintain a permanent file for individual tax clients. This would include final divorce agreements, employment contracts, stock option information, Section 83b elections, alternative minimum tax credit backup, basis calculations, or schedules of carryover amounts. Use a yellow folder for these items.
- *Red "mailbox."* Every client would have a red "mailbox" folder. Any correspondence, mail, or loose papers are filed by the administrative assistant in this folder. When someone goes to work on that client, he or she must first clean out the red folder, dispose of any open items, and properly file everything else. This becomes a communication method to let people working on a client know what is going on.

No loose papers should be permitted in any file when handed in to the reviewer. The only loose items should be a printout of the tax return and an envelope with the client's original information that is to be returned with the completed tax return.

Note that my firm has been paperless for over 10 years and I find it hard to think back to the paper file procedures with all the handling and time spent retrieving, adding information, trying to locate pages, and refiling the folders.

Paperless Procedures

Changing and advancing technology has been vigorously seized by the accounting profession. Spreadsheet software might be the single most important reason why personal computers were purchased, giving rise to mass-produced quantities that made the PC affordable. Then came tax preparation program software, followed by accounting system or bookkeeping programs. Today, we have paperless offices with Cloud-based filing systems, work flow software, smart scanners and e-delivery methods and tax filing.

The reality is that paperless procedures will be a staple in all our offices, so why not get started if you haven't already?

Starting with tax return preparation is actually an easy way to begin. Tax return preparation is a self-contained system. You don't need special software—most tax software has buttons to convert to Adobe PDF files. Tax return preparation has all the work compartmentalized by year, client information, and the return output. Governments want e-filed returns and are even penalizing firms that file paper copies. Clients are adapting to having information e-mailed to them.

Other paperless tax software includes the tax research services. When I started in business, we used to have a librarian come in every other week for a full day of filing the updates. Today, almost everything is online. Even CD-ROMs have disappeared.

To start, all that's needed is a paperless attitude. You have to be focused on being paperless. When in doubt, go paperless. Preplanning should be done, and the process should be carefully organized with the right training and equipment. Note that the cost and time savings and increased confidence a firm can achieve make any initial costs worthwhile.

What we've done is digitize our working paper filing procedures. Previously, when we filed paper documents, reports and copies, we did not make digital or PDF copies and file them on the server. We have "digital" folders for PDF tax return copies, clients' original information, research questions, review notes, flag sheets that contain special or follow-up data or issues when the return is prepared, financial planning, reference letters and other correspondence with and on the behalf of the client, and a permanent file with information such as divorce agreements and closing statements for real estate.

Software exists that puts an index on files and allows you to search for files by key words, dates, and file names; it saves the files as if they resided in your filing cabinet. Some software is Cloud-based, permitting you to access files from anywhere. Files can be password protected, of course.

Note that going paperless is a major undertaking, and it should be carefully planned and organized with the right training and equipment. Jack Welch, writing in *Jack: Straight from the Gut*, said that it doesn't make sense to have a digital system and paper system. Considering the difference in the ongoing costs and efficiency between the two, what are we all waiting for? Note that the start-up costs need to be considered, but our experiences with many CPAs indicate that these are quickly recovered by the efficiencies and ease of using the digital systems.

Part of the paperless protocol is e-filing clients' tax returns. Whatever your reservations, the system works. The time savings are enormous. They include speeding up file retrieval and file use and clutter reduction. It's now faster to open and review files when clients call with questions. None of our clients objected once we explained that it would reduce or eliminate data entry errors by tax agencies and speed their refunds. The cost savings include paper expense; copying charges, including administrative staff time; and postage and overnight charges. You will also reduce file storage space and convert space previously used for file folders into work space, or find that you can manage with smaller offices.

Another aspect of being paperless is using Cloud-based tax preparation programs. These are always up to date and accessible from any location, not just from the office. They also enable staff to occasionally work from home and save traveling or commuting time.

Unrelated to tax season, but integral to an accounting practice, is that audit working papers are Cloud-based and paperless, eliminating the need to carry tons of paper and secure files overnight. The reduced "wear and tear" on staff is certainly worth the cost. Employee training is minimal, with readily intuitive methods and procedures. Windows-based programs contain similar instructions and keystrokes—anyone with a Windows background can easily pick up new software. The only training is in the specific applications of working papers and adherence to firm internal procedures with respect to backing up work and signatures.

Accountants have a history of extensive file folder procedures. However, the paperless system has almost completely eliminated the need for paper file folders. Everything we used and did is now saved on our server and rapidly increasing use of Cloud-based servers. In some respects, you can follow the procedures established for your paper files; it's just that now, all information maintained digitally.

We recommend that every staff person have a personal scanner (preferably automatic feed, high speed) and a second monitor. Having the second monitor helps increase file handling, input, and review. It's now possible to have the clients' scanned original data on one screen and the tax program on the other. In addition, it's easy to put the current tax return on one screen and the prior-year return on the other and compare the two. For the partners, the ability to retrieve files within seconds without leaving their chair speeds up tax return and data retrieval when clients call with questions. Looking at returns on the screen while talking to clients also enables partners to suggest additional services such as financial planning, investment management, or tax planning.

Personal scanners have become such necessities around our office that we wonder how we ever got along without them. In fact, we've invested in portable scanners, allowing us to input data right at the client's office or at our homes. Because staff can hook up to the firm's server from off-site locations, it's literally the same as being at the office. Scanners and monitors are inexpensive; the cost easily recoverable within a few months through increased productivity, less intraoffice chatter, greater efficiency, and faster turnaround time.

Irrespective of how much I like the paperless procedures, staff will still need printers. I have also found separate laser printers becoming popular for each staff person. Usually, centralized printers (many are high speed, but not all) are used office-wide. This requires people who are sending data and returns to the printer to get up to get printouts (actually, the exercise is not too bad for you). We have seen people sending to the printer a 120-page tax return, with copies to be filed with the tax authorities, client, and office files (360 printed pages), and 8 seconds later, someone sends a 2-page memo that is needed for a meeting that he or she is rushing to. How many times do you think the second person ran back to the printer to see if the memo printed? Add to this a couple of other people sending their work to the centralized printer. How much wasted time? Measuring this against the cost of the extra printers in each office. We believe the extra printers win hands down. One other point—suppose someone wanted to print his or her copy on special paper that has to be manually fed into the printer. How can this be done when others can beat you to the printer? One point of organizing for tax season is to provide an efficient method for getting the work done, and that might not always be the conventional or expected way. We vote for 1 printer per person (or per room, with not more than 3 people sharing the printer).

You can use many high-speed and portable scanners. Many of what we used to call photocopiers are now scanners that deliver the digital version to your computer and are also copiers and miniprint centers. You also will need the full version of Adobe Acrobat, with editing, bookmarking, and security features, to transfer your documents into this format. Also, sending a PDF copy captures your styling, formatting, and fonts in the exact way you developed the file.

Our converting to a paperless office truly was a seamless transition. No one had trouble adjusting. Once we rid ourselves of the fear of getting started, we accomplished our goal with lightning speed. When a return is prepared in our paperless environment, a PDF copy can be e-mailed to the client to review, a copy can be kept on the server, and the government copy can be electronically filed. It is truly amazing: not one piece of paper and click, click, click. And so, my fellow CPAs, I leave you with this: when in doubt, go paperless.

Paperless Outsource Alternative

New technology systems are being developed daily to ease the tax preparation process. One example is a "smart" scanner that can read W-2s, K-1s, and 1099s and place the information on the proper line of the tax preparation software.

We started out hesitantly. We now use it firm-wide with some of our offices using it for 90 percent of their returns. They are being improved daily. If you are interested in this time-saving process, look into it or contact me and I will refer you to possible vendors.

Controlling Paperless Systems

Controlling the paperless office is no different from paper procedures. A system must have checks and balances and some redundancy. We used to use a control sheet with space to indicate that a return was saved (or printed) to the paperless filing cabinet. Now we use workflow software which I referred to previously and wholeheartedly recommend.

In tax season, many opportunities exist to check the work because clients continuously call with questions that require staff to retrieve the saved returns and backup information. Everyone must be disciplined enough to track down the person who made the mistake and have him or her correct what he or she did wrong.

One method to follow is that after the return is reviewed for the last time, it is sent to the office staff to process for sending to the client. A staff member will save the return to the paperless filing cabinet and so indicate on the process sheet. When the return is given to the partner to sign, he or she makes sure it has been filed on the server. If not, it is returned to the office staff for that to be done.

For any system to be effective, it must be followed, and those who don't follow it, have to be told to correct his or her omissions. The omissions should not be corrected by the next person handling the file or the person catching the omission.

Bookmarking

File, working paper, and documentation organization is paramount for an effective system. The few minutes extra time organizing the data could save hours at a later time. Also, the few minutes is usually done by a staff or administrative person, but the hours is done by a senior manager or partner and is more than likely done while they are being challenged by the client. Any method that works uniformly throughout the firm is okay.

Following is a listing of standard bookmarking for paperless systems. If you aren't paperless yet, you can print sets of lead sheets with each index item as a heading. We did this with the heading printed on the bottom left of the page. We also printed sets of file folder labels and pasted the labels on the bottom of the back-up information we copied and retained or on the copies we made or scanned. Today, with "smart" scanners and software, the bookmarking is automatic. I think the order is important, so people going through the file will have a familiarity even if they have no prior knowledge of the client's situation. Good order creates ease for other preparers who might need to work on that file, reviewers, partners, and clients if they need to receive copies of your backup. Occasionally, we copy our backup onto a CD and give it to the client so that he or she does not need to retain the hard paper copies. At other times, we give clients access to our files through our client portal. When a client sees your working papers, he or she will form an opinion of how you work: neat and orderly or disorganized and sloppy. It is your call.

Standard Bookmarking for 1040s

Client Notes

- Income
- W-2s
- Interest income
- Dividend income
- State tax refunds
- Schedule C
- Schedule D
- Schedule D gross proceeds reconciliation worksheet
- Consolidated 1099s
- IRA and pension distributions (1099-Rs)
- Rental real estate or royalty income, or both
- K-1s
- Unemployment compensation
- Social Security income
- Other income

Adjustments to Income

- Simplified employee pension (SEP) plan and IRA contributions
- Self-employed health insurance
- Student loan interest
- Tuition
- Other adjustments to income

Itemized Deductions

- Medical expenses
- Real estate taxes
- Mortgage interest (1098s)
- Investment interest (margin interest)
- Charitable contributions
- Unreimbursed employee business expenses (2106)
- Other miscellaneous expenses

Credits

- Child or dependent care credit
- Other credits

Other

- Tax payment worksheet
- Tax organizer

Call to Becoming Paperless

This chapter covers paper and paperless procedures. As I edit the copy from the previous edition, I am amazed how much handling and work went into the paper systems and how much was eliminated by being paperless. I strongly recommend the conversion if you haven't switched yet. You are welcome to contact me if you want to discuss or if you need a push.

Prepare the Return 12

This chapter covers several procedures related to preparing a tax return. These procedures include sign-in, working paper, administrative, pro forma, and projection. Note that there is some repetition of information that appeared in other chapters. This has been done so that each chapter has all the information in it on the topics covers and you do not have to go back to prior chapters.

Sign-In Procedures

Old procedures: When work on a return starts, a memo sheet is provided to our administrative assistant for entering the start date on the tax control. This enables the monitoring of follow-up. The memo sheet will be included with every client's submitted tax information. A few times per day, the completed and delivered tax returns are marked off on the tax control and a new list is generated.

New procedures: Using workflow software every touch is recorded in the system and when someone completes his or her work and sends it on, that is indicated in the system and an email message is sent to the next person that it has been passed to the new person. An administrative assistant monitors the system to make sure there is no lag in accepting and starting work on the return. Status reports can be looked at any time by everyone in the system. This is certainly much more effective that the paper system and procedures which I was so proud of when they were developed and adopted by us.

Working Paper Procedures

Even though we now have a paperless system, we still need working papers—only they are not done on paper. Working papers must follow an index sequence (for example, salaries, interest, and dividends). Copies of all 1099s should be kept with related working papers. K-1s should be filed in the proper place, again following an index sequence. All entries on the tax return need support and documentation. This includes amounts received through telephone inquiry, which must be documented in the file in the proper place. In some instances, a notation of a discussion with the client is sufficient.

All working papers should be indexed and labeled. The indexing must be accomplished by the proper use of the individual tax return index. The index was designed to be flexible and easy to use. It also highlights mandatory forms, such as the "Individual Tax Return Checklist." An item may have more than one working paper number assigned to it (for example, dividend income 6A–6C), but either the top sheet of that section or a lead sheet must have a total of the items that tie into the tax return total.

If the organizer (systematizer) is the source of a particular item, enter an *S* on the working paper number line and the page number on the organizer. Several blank lines at the bottom of the index are for items not listed.

Indicate the basis of presumptions (estimates) used in completing the return in the proper place. If not sure of propriety of basis or entry, the reviewer should speak to a partner before completing the return.

All working papers should be signed and dated by the preparer.

We track tax agency notices very carefully and try to do extra work in the preparation in order to avoid clients getting notices. Working papers are designed with that in mind. Some of the things we do that tremendously reduce the flow of notices are as follows:

- Prepare an extensive worksheet for estimated tax payments. We now ask for copies of the checks or bank statements showing the cleared check or payment.
- Have detailed explanations on the returns for unusual items.
- Do a verification of IRA and pension rollovers, as well as a comparison of last year's 1099s with the ones received this year. If none this year, ask client for an explanation.
- Report incorrect 1099s in the proper place on the return and then subtract the same amount on a different line and document this in the working papers.
- Do a reconciliation of the gross income from the 1099s on a Schedule C, making sure the gross income is equal to or less than the amount reported.

- Make sure the gross security sales on the tax return are at least equal to the amounts on the brokerage firm 1099s.
- Include answers to every question on the return.

We try to do everything in a user-friendly, time-efficient manner. Whenever we set up a new procedure, we give it a user-friendly test. This involves asking if it will be user friendly in terms of making it easier for the client to be our client. We ask if what we are doing will be user friendly to the client when he or she reviews what was done. We try to keep in mind that we are offering a premium-priced, handholding type of service and not running a discount store bargain basement.

In keeping with the neatness kick, every worksheet in the individual files has the client's name and the year laser printed on every page. Also, at the bottom right, is space for the title of the worksheet and the page number.

Working papers are assembled by the preparer, and the information is entered directly into the computer without input sheets.

If there is missing information, a draft federal return is run and kept with the file.

Administrative Procedures

We try to have as few people as possible handle the files, but a minimum of six people always handle them: the administrative person; the interviewer or person receiving the tax information; the preparer; a reviewer; a partner (either the tax, engagement, or contact partner); and the person "pushing the button" for e-filing. With so many people involved, administrative processes become all the more valuable. A few administrative procedures tips are listed here:

- Whenever tax information comes in, an administrative person should record it into the tax control or workflow software.
- The documentation is scanned or put in a special filing cabinet where all in-process tax returns are kept.
- An accountant should assign the returns.
- If the returns are not assigned but are picked on a first in first out (FIFO) basis by the preparer, the person overseeing the selections can be an administrative person.

- A tax calendar should be maintained. Ideally, this should be part of the tax preparation or workflow software and should be maintained by an administrative person. The calendar should be updated daily and either kept on the network or made available to everyone needing to see and use it. With workflow software, this is instantly available.
- Clients who mail in their information should be called to notify them it has arrived safely.
- Everyone touching the file and working on the return should log in the return's progress stage. With workflow software, this becomes a routine step.
- All files in process should be put in special filing cabinets. This enables other personnel to quickly locate a file and complete a return, if necessary. It also provides a place to locate the client's original information, should that be necessary.
- When a return is completed and the final reviewer has signed off on the return, it should be given to the administrative staff to assemble and get ready to send to the client.
- If a bill is to be sent with the return, the final reviewer should either have it prepared (the easiest way would be with the tax preparation software) or ask the signing partner the amount of the fee. Alternatively, the bill will be prepared at the beginning of the next month when the time run is reviewed.
- An administrative person should enter the completed return in the digital filing cabinet when he or she prints it to be assembled.
- The printing should be from the tax preparation software, not from copies; this removes a handling step.
- An administrative person should scan the indexed and properly ordered client's original information (without bookmarking) before it is returned to the client.
- The client's information should be put in an appropriately marked envelope when it is sent back to the client.
- Everything that will be sent to the client should be given to the partner who will sign the return; the partner will give it a final look and signature and "put it in the envelope."
- An alternative is for the signing partner to see and sign the return before it is fully processed to send to the client. Then, the administrative staff will complete processing, binding, and sending the

return. An upside to this method is that the partner will get a look before the return is assembled and bound. A downside is that the partner will not see the final package as it will be sent to the client.

- Someone—an administrative person—should follow up on a regular basis with clients to make sure we get the e-filing forms returned timely. This should start no later than one week after the return has been sent out of our office and can continue at three- to four-day intervals. Delegating this task will prevent bottlenecks from developing during the last week of tax season and relieve an accountant or preparer from getting involved. Also, when an accountant calls, clients tend to ask questions, such as how much do they have to pay, how much is their refund, or was the fourth corrected form picked up on their return. An administrative person will spend much less time on those calls.

Pro Forma Procedures

Regardless of paper or paperless preparation, proformas and carryover data must be reviewed before working on a return. Check that the spelling of client's name and his or her address and Social Security number are correct.

We have a place on our tax control sheet to indicate whether proformas from last year were used. This makes it easier for the reviewer and allows him or her to only spot check the data, rather than check each item separately.

Projection Procedures

It is always easier to do something later or tomorrow or some other time, especially during tax season. However, the nature of public accounting is that we are always busy, and generally, some degree of pressure always exists, meaning that there is no "best" time to do something. Overlooking the special time-crunching circumstances of tax season, the most propitious time to prepare the projections is when the tax return is worked on. Time is a fungible asset—if you have to do it and you don't do it today, you will still have to spend the time doing it. That being said, you'll spend the least amount of time on projections when you have the client's file open and you are working intensely on his or her individual tax return. An added benefit of doing it at that time is easing the review and oversight process, as well as having the projection available in real time to discuss with the client. You can also plan for opportunities to be proactive with the client to reduce his or her tax or plan for the cash needed to pay the estimated taxes.

Projections are prepared using specialized tax projection programs. The information must be entered separately from the tax preparation software, causing additional work. You can also use many tax preparation programs that have "add tos" and "subtraction froms" to prepare the estimated taxes for the current year. However, much of the tax preparation software's output is over 20 pages, with summary sheets that do not show the data in a user-friendly manner.

We use projections as a review tool. The actual numbers on the final return are compared with the projection for that year and also for the next year. The reviewer will also eyeball the actual amounts from the prior two or three years. The preparer is advised to perform these steps before handing in the return for review. It is always better for the preparer, rather than the reviewer, to find errors.

This pre review process by the preparer allows the preparer to take a few moments to look at the big picture and reflect on any tax planning or financial planning possibilities for the client. Even if it is too late for planning for the return that was just prepared or the year that just ended, the planning can be recommended for the current year or later years.

Also, we will use projections for pre-year-end meetings with clients. So, you must think in terms of making it easier for the client to be your client. Ask yourself if what you are doing will be user friendly for the clients when they review what was done. Keep in mind that you are offering a Nordstrom-type handholding service, not a Kmart self-service operation.

A few tips on projections are as follows:

- When pre reviewing the return by comparing it with, and possibly reconciling it to, the projection, you should not overlook the opportunity to save the client tax dollars for the past year or to apply for refunds for the previous two years.
- The projections done while you are preparing the return should be done on the tax preparation software. If the projections are done any other time, they should be done using the tax projection software.

- Summaries of the projections are entered on an Excel spreadsheet. The object is to have user-friendly information to give to clients or use at client meetings. The better the presentation, the more substance that will be covered at the meeting.
- One thing we do to present information so that the client can relate to it is grouping all the items on a K-1 together on the Excel spreadsheet. We do not put interest income from a K-1 with the Schedule B items because doing so only causes confusion when a client reviews the summary. Clients never think of the individual parts of the K-1s; they only know the net result.
- You should also prepare extensive comparative multiyear spreadsheets for Schedule C businesses and Schedule E rental properties, K-1s, interest and dividend income, and similar information that is reported on the current tax return, as well as the prior years' returns. This is also very helpful in our review process, and a big help to the client who receives copies, because it gives a quick summary of business or rental property activity and a basis of comparison.
- You should also prepare detailed stock options (both ISO and NQSO) and restricted stock schedules. Also, for clients who are insiders with stock options and restricted stock, you can look up their transactions on the Internet because the Securities and Exchange Commission tracks these activities.
- For clients with K-1s in which we have access to their cash flow information, we include cash flow information on the K-1 schedules.
- For clients without K-1s and who have multiple accounts, any property or Schedule Cs, you can use the two-year comparison tax preparation software printouts. Also, print out all the tax preparation software backup worksheets for your review and to be available when you meet with the client, but do not give them to the client.
- Clients who have C corporations with retained earnings should be asked if they want us to project taxes on dividends. This could be very helpful for clients anticipating a low income year.
- We give each client a spreadsheet containing annual summaries of his or her tax return for the previous four to six years. When applicable, we also provide a projection of the next year (that is, the current year).

- We provide summaries of all of the client's K-1s organized by the various components of income expense items. We also provide from four to five years of summaries of Schedule E and Schedule C.
- When applicable, we provide summaries of the client's interest and dividend income by account and payer. We also prepare a distribution analysis of taxability by federal tax and each state in which the client is subject to tax. This also makes it much easier for the return to be reviewed.
- We also provide an analysis of tax loss carryforwards (Schedule E, rental property items, capital gains, business operating losses, charity deductions, and alternative minimum tax credit availability).

Sample Individual Tax Return Office and Administrative Procedures

Note: XCM is the workflow tracking system we use. GFR refers to our paperless file system. There are many other products on the market that you can also check out. I strongly recommend both concepts—workflow software and paperless filing systems.

1. When a client's tax documents are received, please let the tax administrator know and he or she will log them into XCM to the "Unassigned" step. The documents should then be put in the appropriate drawer outside the tax manager's office.
   a. A partner or manager may put a note in XCM if it should be assigned to a specific preparer.
2. An admin person will scan the information into our system using the smart scanner.
3. The preparer will take the next return either from XCM or from the right of the drawer marked "To Be Prepared" (no exceptions). Because some returns may be automatically assigned by the tax managers to tax preparers, all staff should check their XCM "My View" folder daily.

4. The first thing that the preparer must do is to go into XCM, search for the client, and move the tax return (task) to the "Preparation" step and assign it to himself or herself.
5. The preparer will
   a. review the scanned documents and the way the information was entered into the tax program
   b. prepare the tax return.
   c. set up all required state returns (jurisdictions) in XCM (if they have not already been set up). Also make sure that the year-end is correct on the XCM folder and that the due dates are correct for all federal and state forms.
   d. use and fill out all required checklists and worksheets.
   e. compare the current tax return with the prior year tax return.
   f. set up the return for e-filing, do a full recompute, and create the e-file.
   g. clear all diagnostics and e-file rejects.
   h. review on screen the completed tax return for obvious errors.
6. The preparer will make a list of open items in XCM. To do this, go to the "Issues/Points" tab and enter your questions or missing information. Then, click on "Send to CPA Responsible." This may be the partner or manager or other responsible person. The preparer should follow up every few days with the partner or manager. (If there aren't any open items then skip the next two steps.)

(continued)

7. In XCM, the tax return is now at the step "Questions Posted" and is assigned to the person responsible to get the questions answered or obtain the missing information. If at this point, the responsible person wants to assign another person, or the preparer, to obtain the missing information, he or she should move the task in XCM to that person and keep it at the "Questions Posted" step.
8. Once all of the open items are received, the partner or manager or other person responsible will go into XCM to the "Issues/Points" tab and click on "Send to Preparer." The return is now assigned back to the preparer to the step "Questions Answered." At this point, the preparer must finish the tax return as soon as possible.
9. The preparer will go into XCM and move the tax return to the step "Unassigned Awaiting Review." A printed copy of the return will not be given to the reviewers. All review of the tax returns will be done on screen. Put the tax documents in the designated area for returns awaiting assignment. If the tax return is preassigned to a specific reviewer, then give the tax documents to that person.
10. The tax return will be assigned to a reviewer. Either a tax manager will assign the return to a specific reviewer and will move it to him or her in XCM or a reviewer will assign himself or herself to the return that has been at the step "Unassigned Awaiting Review" the longest and will move it to the "Review" step.

11. The reviewer will take the tax documents from the designated holding place. The reviewer will review the tax return and enter review notes into XCM in the "Issues/Points—Review Points" tab. The reviewer will make sure that all forms (jurisdictions) being filed are set up in XCM with the correct due dates and will indicate which returns will be e-filed. The reviewer will make sure that the tax working papers were saved in GFR and bookmarked and all required checklists and worksheets were prepared. The reviewer will move the return to the step "Open Review Points" and assign it back to the preparer to clear all review notes. The reviewer will not give the tax documents back to the preparer at this point.
12. The preparer will clear all of the review notes, move the tax return to the step "Cleared Review Points," and assign it back to the reviewer.
13. The reviewer will do a full recompute, create the e-file, and make sure that there aren't any e-filing rejects. He or she will print the tax return. The reviewer will mark the milestone complete and enter the completed date in the tax software. The reviewer will give the tax return and tax documents to the partner signing the return. In XCM, the reviewer will move the tax return to the step "Signer Review" and will assign it to the signer or partner.
14. The signer or partner will review and sign the tax return and put it into the administrative drawer for processing. In XCM, the partner or signer will indicate the method of delivery in the shipping tab, as well as any other special instructions. The partner or signer will go into XCM, move the tax return to the step "To Be Assembled," and leave the "Assigned (Moved) To Whom" box blank. If the signer has any changes to the return he or she will follow the same procedures as the reviewer under step 12.

(continued)

15. The person who processes the return will go into XCM, keep the tax return at the "To Be Assembled" step, and assign it to himself or herself. He or she will check assembly and shipping instructions and prepare to send accordingly. The tax return will be assembled and scanned into GFR by the administrative department. They will go into XCM and move it to the step "To Be Signed" and assign it back to the partner or signer. They will give the assembled tax return back to the partner or signer. If the return will be sent by an overnight delivery service, they will also give the partner or signer the envelope and slip.
16. The partner or signer will check the assembly; sign the return; and put the assembled tax return in the mail, overnight service, and so on. In XCM, he or she will move it to the step "To Be Shipped" and assign it to tax administrator.
17. The e-filer will be responsible for obtaining the signed e-file authorization forms from the clients. Once the e-filer receives the signed authorization forms, he or she will submit the electronic file in Go System. The e-filer will follow up to make sure the e-file was accepted. In XCM, the e-filer will choose the proper steps for the e-filing process.

Worksheet for Federal and State Tax Payments and State Tax Deduction

STATE INCOME TAX DEDUCTION
FEDERAL & STATE TAX PAYMENTS

Client: ______________________ Year: __________

	Federal	NJ	NYS	NYC	SUI/SDI	Other
Withholdings:						
Withholdings per W-2s:						
Employer:						
Other Withholdings (Int., Div., 1099s, K-1s, Excess FICA and SUI/SDI, and so on):						
Source:						
NJ Excess SYU/SDI		-				
Total Withholdings	-	-	-	-	-	-
Estimated tax payments for ______:						
Credit applied from prior year return: (if did itemized in prior year, calculate if should be picked up as income)						
4/15/20XX						
6/15/20XX						
9/15/20XX						
12/31/20XX						
1/15/20XY						
Total Estimated Tax Payments	-	-	-	-	-	-
Total W/H, Estimates, and Ext Pymts	-	-	-	-	-	-

(continued)

	Federal	NJ	NYS	NYC	SUI/SDI	Other
Additional payments						
4th Qtr. 20WW Est. pd. in Jan. 20XX						
Balance Due for 'WW (Pd. in 'XX)						
WW State Refund Attrib to Taxes Paid in 'XX						
Other Payments (explain)						
Less: 4th Qtr. 'WW pd Jan. 'YY		-	-	-	-	-
Less: Extension Pmt. Pd. in 'YY			-	-	-	-
Total Deduction on Federal Return		-	-	-	-	-
Grand Total Deduction on Federal Return of all State Taxes			-			

Were the estimated tax payments and extension payments verified with cancelled checks? Yes/No __________

If answer to above question is "No," how were payments verified? Explain __________

Worksheet to Reconcile Forms 1099-B and 1099-S to Tax Returns

RECONCILIATION OF FORMS 1099-B AND 1099-S

Client Name:______________________________

Year:__________

Proceeds From Stocks, Bonds, and so on and Real Estate Sales:

Name of Broker	Amount
Total	$ –

Total Sales Price Amounts Reported on Schedule D:

Line	Amount
3	
10	
Total	$ –

Note:

If the total amount reported on Schedule D is less than the total amount reported on Form 1099, attach a statement to the tax return explaining the difference or note the difference below.

Review the Return 13

Reviewing tax returns is a key part of tax preparation. It also is an area vulnerable to major bottlenecks and backlogs. Tax return reviews are performed by more highly skilled professionals who are more difficult to train or find. Therefore, you must consider anything that can be done to reduce review time.

This chapter covers methods to reduce review time, establish who should conduct the review, determine content versus issue review, identify specific items for the reviewer to check, and establish administrative procedures.

Methods to Reduce Review Time

To have a successful tax season, care and effort must be spent to reduce the review time while maintaining quality. The reviewer's time is the main element that needs to be managed and reduced. Some ways this can be accomplished are included in the following box.

General Procedures

- Better training of the preparers
- Better training of the reviewers
- Digitization as much as possible, such as reviewing the returns on the screen and reducing printing and paper handling; reviewing the backup on an indexed digital file; electronically transferring K-1s when the corporate, partnership, or trust return is prepared by the firm; carrying forward carryover and pro forma data kept track of by the tax preparation software; filling out client organizers online and transferring them into the current year's program

(continued)

- Modularization or compartmentalization of the work so it can be done and reviewed more easily
- Better scheduling of the work so the more complicated returns are not bunched together and can be reviewed calmly and separately instead of being bunched together when they reach the reviewer
- Creating a less harried, less hurried office atmosphere
- Keeping everything in order and in its place

Preparer Procedures

- Compare the completed return to last year's return and make sure there are no great differences.
- Use the tax comparison feature to compare last year's categories with this year's. Note that many preparers might do a diligent job of entering information and tying in all their work, but they neglect to look at the return they just completed. Experienced reviewers easily uncover many errors by simply looking at the output and also comparing it with the previous year's return. Getting the preparer to do this first would raise the quality of the finished product passed on to the reviewer and reduce the reviewer's time, the error correction time, and the total processing and handling time.
- For complicated returns, prepare an Excel comparison worksheet separating the K-1 information from the various parts of the return in which the information appears, such as in interest, capital gains, Section 179 depreciation, tax credits, and perhaps Schedule E activities. This makes comparing the client's activities and return easier. Refer to chapter 10 to learn how the Excel worksheets should be prepared.
- Use uniform procedures and worksheets wherever possible. Anticipate the reviewer's process and create worksheets and schedules that will tie into the amounts on the tax return so the preparer can easily see the work product and be able to quickly test the transactions. Prepare worksheets that reconcile amounts that must be correct because the programs of the IRS and tax authorities tie out with the information they have.

- Look at the output and compare it with any projection that was done for the client to last year's tax return and the tax comparisons from the preparation software (how you enforce this requirement is a function of your training and quality control programs).
- Before passing the return to the reviewer, respond to all open items in the software diagnostics so that there are no items left for the reviewer to resolve or follow up on.
- Read and complete the checklists.
- Have another preparer prereview the detail input. Having a person at the same level as the preparer review the input will push the work down from the reviewer, will serve to help the same level reviewer hone his or her skills at locating the types and frequency of errors, and might create peer pressure to not have someone at the same level find the errors.

Added effort by the preparer will save reviewers' time. We have found that requiring extensive, complete, neat, organized, and indexed working papers or PDF files will take about 20 minutes per return but will reduce the time it takes the preparer to prepare a return by approximately 80 minutes—net gain: 1 hour per return. For a workload of 400 returns, this reduces the time by the equivalent of 1 full time person during tax season.

The following refers to paper systems. Smart scanners will do a lot of this work before it reaches the preparer. A method that can be used is to have the preparer put the clients' information in order, with indexed cover sheets placed before each group. A cover sheet could also contain an adding machine tape or spreadsheet tying in the original data. The person scanning the data could scan everything without bookmarking, provided that an index is prepared by the preparer indicating the order of the information and a letter index is put on the top (or bottom) of each page. This will make it a little harder to find information saved on the server, but that will usually be done after the return has been completed, saving time during the busy season. The only time it will be referred to will be if a question arises after filing and when next year's return is being prepared. This may be a lower-cost way to put the information into the server, balanced by the little extra time it would take to find something if later questions about the file arise.

The reason organizing works is that many people, especially less experienced preparers, are not always clear on how they should start when presented with the clients' "shopping bag" of data. The method of having the original data copied or scanned and indexed provides a starting point and method of getting going. Also, we are unleashing brain power. By handling every bit of data, the brain captures the information and is already assembling it in the proper order, so you have a head start when you actually commence the input. Note that new software and scanners are replacing the manual bookmarking and entering the data from W-2s, 1099s, and certain K-1s. The scanning can be done by administrative personnel and reviewed by the preparer. This upgrades the preparer's function and involves administrative people more in the preparation process.

Besides having excellent working papers with a shorter overall preparation time, even greater benefits are derived by having the tax department spend less time reviewing a return while substantially raising the quality of the review. The tax department, on some level, has a finite amount of time available for review, but the preparation staff might have infinite time because it is much easier to hire tax return preparers than reviewers.

Another benefit is a selfish one and one that every partner personally benefits from: the ease of reviewing a file and discussing a tax return matter with a client.

This is especially important if a return is sent out with an error. The partner, who has to explain the error to a client, can quickly retrieve the inputted data. Clear working papers and ease of retrieval can literally make the difference in keeping or losing the client.

Another benefit, and a very important one, is that neat, orderly working papers or PDF files also create a more professional attitude among the staff.

Who Should Conduct the Review?

The main decision about who should conduct the review is between the tax department, which would review every tax return, or other higher-level personnel (such as audit managers and partners) who might not necessarily have the comprehensive training, background, and experience to handle everything that might come up during the tax preparation process. Generally, the tax department has limited staff, and the concentration of work places an almost insurmountable burden on that staff. Additionally, in most firms, almost everyone on the staff will prepare some returns, and that lack of dedicated preparation skills will place an added burden on the tax department during their review process.

Reviewer Qualification Test

Following are 10 questions reviewers should be able to answer in order to qualify as a reviewer. Regardless of whether you agree with the following questions, you have to consider a method of making sure the reviewers are qualified. Doing so will also include reviewer-appropriate continuing professional education and in-house training.

1. What is the latest date a simplified employee pension (SEP) plan can be opened for 20XX for a sole proprietor?
2. What date is used as the purchase date to report a stock transaction that includes an unallowed loss because there was a previous wash sale?
3. Are extra payments made to an ex-spouse to cover unanticipated increases in tuition in his or her nursing school deductible as alimony?
4. What is the maximum federal capital gains tax rate from any portion of the gain on commercial real estate that an individual tax client sells?
5. When would you use the annualization exception for the 2210 penalty?
6. How are Section 1256 gains taxed?
7. How would you advise a client who gives large amounts of annual charitable contributions and typically has large long-term capital gains?

(continued)

8. What cost basis is used when a client sells enough restricted stock shares at the point of vesting to cover the taxes on his or her employer's restricted stock shares granted three years earlier and the stock broker has provided a 1099 showing proceeds of $12,100?
9. What would be a minimum strategy for a client with incentive stock options to avoid the alternative minimum tax?
10. What is the equivalent taxable interest amount for a client with 4 percent municipal bond interest if his or her marginal federal tax rate is 25 percent (assume no state tax)?

Content Versus Issue Review

Each type of review requires a different discipline. The two primary types of reviews are content and issues.

In a content review, the preparer checks most or all of the original client information and determines whether it has been entered and used correctly. This review is very time consuming, and although a lower-level staff person can do it, a tax department specialist usually performs the review. We find that this type of review does not add value. It might improve the accuracy of the return, but it doesn't make the client richer.

An issues review purely adds value. Not only are tax issues examined to see if they are applicable, but the focus is also on planning for the current year and finding ways to make the client richer.

In an ideal world, everything that should be done would be done, with the proper time allowed for each step. Also, preparers and reviewers must understand that the tax return must be properly prepared—with the input carefully and correctly entered; with an understanding of what information might be missing; with tax savings, planning, and compliance issues deliberately considered; and with "outside the box" planning considered, such as financial, retirement, or family security issues developed or brought to the clients' attention as the return is being prepared and reviewed by the accounting firm.

Now, back to reality. Any human endeavor has errors. The issue becomes one of where you want the errors to occur: in missing a charity receipt or overlooking an opportunity to provide advice on opening a SEP plan, contributing to a Roth IRA, enrolling in an employer's 401(k) plan, or choosing the types of mutual funds for the client. By the way, the proper handling of errors also can be opportunities for the firm. If the error is quickly identified, acknowledged, and rectified, the client often will gain a greater confidence in the firm than if the error hadn't been made. However, we do not recommend this as a method of client bonding.

Review Procedures Equal Quality Control

If you think quality control (QC), do you look at tax return reviews differently?

From my speaking to accountants across the country, it is my understanding that the review time is approximately 40 percent of the time it takes the preparer to do the return (not considering calls to get additional information and error correcting time). Consider your clients that have QC departments. How much time do you think they spend on average for QC? Would 5 percent seem right? Accounting firms that have a high review time usually have high error rates, necessitating the high review time. Doesn't that sound crazy? Why not set up procedures to reduce the error rate?

Quality Control Checklist

Here are some comments and questions to ask yourself:

1. Quality control (QC) should represent reality, not theoretical wants or would like to haves.
2. Who is responsible QC?
   a. The reviewer
   b. The partner
   c. The preparer
   d. The person assembling the return
   e. The client
   f. The IRS or tax agency
3. Who does the QC at your firm?
   a. How many returns have errors that are found by the person signing the return?
   b. How many errors are found by the assembler?
   c. How many errors are found by the client?
   d. How many errors are found by the tax agency?
4. Do preparers check their work?
   a. ☐ "Yes" ☐ "No"
   b. What percentage of a preparer's returns have errors found by the reviewer?
   ☐ 25% ☐ 50% ☐ 75% ☐ 95%
   c. How do preparers check their work?
      i. Do they fill out the preparer's checklist?
      ii. Do they clear all the diagnostic questions?
      iii. Do they look at the completed return before handing it in for review?
      iv. Do they compare the completed return with last year's return?
      v. Do they compare the return with the projection that was done?
      vi. Do they fill out an "Ed Mendlowitz Excel Comparison Sheet?"
      vii. Do they separately calculate the tax?

viii. Do they look at size of the refund or balance due to see if it looks reasonable?

ix. What do you do to check yourself when you prepare a return?

The section following this one deals with the quality of a self-review. The reasons for doing so should be obvious: it will reduce overall time, conserve the reviewers' time, and create a more efficient process.

5. When the partner gets the return to sign and he or she finds an error, whose error is it?
   a. ☐ The preparer's ☐ The reviewer's

In my opinion, it is the reviewer's error. The reviewer's job is to find the errors before passing on the return.

6. Are the checklists filled out deliberately, carefully, and correctly?
   a. By ☐ the preparer ☐ the reviewer ☐ anyone else ☐ anyone

How Effective Self-Reviews Improve Efficiency

It occurs to me that there is a difference in the quality between the returns that someone does for himself or herself and the ones done for his or her clients.

An informal survey that I conducted showed that the percentage of returns with errors of sole practitioners and partners in CPA firms is less than 2 percent, but the percentage of errors by their staff ranges from a low of 30 percent to a high of 95 percent. Why the difference?

It seems that there are two primary reasons:

- Knowing that someone will check everything.
- Knowing that no one will check the work.

I don't believe that work is done as carefully if it is known that someone will be rechecking everything that was done. Following are some ways to use this knowledge to have the returns better prepared by staff and use the reviewers more effectively:

- One way to solve this problem is to not recheck everything (usually referred to as *ticking and tying*) but to let it be known that there will only be spot checks or brief but selective overviews.
- Another way is to have the preparer tie in everything and close off the working papers by assuming everything is perfect and will need no changes. This will cause a big annoyance and much more work if errors are found. However, by using this method, I have seen that the quality of the preparers' work is greatly improved, with much less time being spent by reviewers and much lower overall time spent on the return, albeit the extra inconvenience and cost of reopening the closed files. The objective is a better return with quicker turnaround and higher quality, and that is usually the result. The higher quality comes from the reviewers being better able to look for issues and planning opportunities, rather than errors in arithmetic on grouping sheets and missed charity deductions. Note that this method is for returns done by people competent to do the work and not people you are training or teaching; however, this method can be adapted to any level of preparer.

- A third way is to delegate the ticking and tying (if you must do it) to a peer preparer before the return is turned in to the reviewer.

I have used all three of these methods, and they all result in a better product, less cost, and quicker turnaround than a method whereby the reviewer rechecks everything. Another method that I have recently begun advocating is to change the name of the review department to the quality control department. I believe this will decrease the error rate because of QC's connotation. Also, everyone knows that the QC people rarely recheck everything.

Knowing that no one will recheck the tax return causes a much more deliberate and thorough self-review. Proof of this is the small amount of errors made by people preparing their own tax returns. *Errors on a return* is defined by either a tax agency notice being sent to correct or call attention to an error, finding an error yourself after the return has been filed, such as when you are preparing a subsequent year's return, or a client noticing an error when he or she receives his or her return.

Assuming I am correct, if a system could be initiated to have the preparers in a firm do a better job of reviewing their own work before handing it in, then overall quality will be improved, and once again, you will be reducing the most dear time during tax season—that of the reviewers—oops, that of the QC people.

None of the preceding involves additional teaching or training in taxes, but it does require a major change in the preparer's mindset. If I might suggest, it requires a change of culture to that of extremely low tolerance for errors. This change generally starts at the top and works its way down, so the partners need buy in to it before you start. Partner buy-in is the best way to begin new initiatives. I recommend adopting what I have suggested, but before doing so, you will need to get all the partners to agree to adhere to the policy and you need to appoint a champion to oversee the implementation. Everyone should have the same goal: to make more money, have happier and better served clients and staff functioning at the highest levels they are able to. If so, then why is there resistance to change after it is agreed to?

In some instances, I have seen highly improved QC, with isolated reviewers who take the time to insist that prepares give them good work. They set the standard and teach it one on one to those who will be passing work to them. Usually, this change starts with consternation but results in better work all around, happier staff, and a high quality return for the client.

My challenge to you is to consider your internal procedures and decide if you are satisfied with them. If so, then good for you. However, if you believe a change is in order, why not consider what I said previously and try it? We should all be on the same page—to want better turnaround, a higher quality return because of fewer preparer errors (the preparers understand that the review won't be as thorough, so they do a better initial job) and more focused issue reviews, which is really the best way to use the reviewers' brains, experience, and training.

Checklist for the Reviewer

It is important to remember that part of the training process is for the preparer, not the reviewer, to make any necessary changes, even though it might be a simple change.

A re-review is performed before the return is copied and assembled. The return is reviewed once again by the tax partner and finally by the partner who signs it.

The tax projection that has been prepared is reviewed by the tax partner to determine if the return is on target with the projection and information that were given to the client back in October, November, or December. Notes are also made about planning opportunities for the client.

The following is a checklist of things for the reviewer (some items can be test checked):

- The client's name and address
- Social Security numbers
- Estimated tax payments
- K-1 input
- W-2 input
- 1099 input
- Gross sales from security transactions
- Addbacks and reductions of items for state tax returns
- Items on flag sheets entered
- Diagnostics and no open or unresolved items

- All questions on the preparer's checklist answered by preparer
- Special instructions on the control sheet followed
- That repetitively incorrect issues are looked at and included on the checklist (such as opportunities for IRA or SEP plan contributions, clients' ages and Social Security numbers, and ages of dependents)
- Opportunities for tax planning for the client

Each January, I prepare an updated version of a Reviewer's Check List for Individual Returns and one for Business Returns. You are welcome to email me for the latest versions in a Word file you can adapt if you wish. I will also include other tax season checklists and updates to any checklists, forms or templates in this book. Email me at emendlowitz@withum.com. There is no charge. Just mention this book.

Administrative Procedures

In many firms, tax preparers or reviewers have to perform multiple administrative-related procedures. Following are some tasks that can best be performed by appropriate administrative staff, freeing the preparers or reviewers to do what they do best:

- Printing paper copies of the completed return and then giving them to the administrative staff to copy, further assemble, and get ready to be sent to the client
- Entering the completed, fully reviewed return to the server
- Organizing the clients' original information that is to be returned
- Making sure special filing instructions are adhered to
- Signing the returns (this might be better done by someone else, either a partner or another reviewer, giving a person unrelated to the preparation an opportunity to have a fresh look at the return)

Answers to Reviewer Qualification Test

1. The due date including extension for the return claiming the deduction.
2. The date the original shares were purchased.
3. Not deductible. Alimony payments must be in a written agreement.
4. Pre-1987 recaptured depreciation is taxed at ordinary income rates; 1987 or later recaptured depreciation on real estate is taxed for 2014 reporting at a top capital gains rate of 25 percent and might be subject to the additional 3.8 percent net investment income tax.
5. When the income is earned erratically, bunched, or not received or paid equally during the year and the annualization results in a lower or no 2210 penalty.
6. Gains are taxed as 60 percent long-term capital gains and 40 percent short-term capital gains regardless of holding period.
7. The client should consider donating appreciated long-term owned securities. The client would get a tax deduction for the full fair market value of the stock and not have to report the capital gain.
8. The employer is required to report the entire gain as wages on the employee's W-2. I would use $12,100. The technically correct answer is the basis is the fair market value on the date vested before deduction for broker's commission. A practical solution is to use the proceeds reported on the W-2 as long as the stock is sold right after the vesting trigger.
9. To consider exercising as much of the ISOs as the client can to the point where the AMT would kick in.
10. 5.33 percent. Divide 4 percent by 75 percent.

Prepare the Bill 14

I believe that the most efficient time to bill is when you send the tax return to the client because the return and client information are in front of you. Also, if you want to ask questions of anyone who worked on the return, it will still be fresh in their minds. Furthermore, clients have the results of your work, along with their pile of information, in their hands when they see your bill. They are writing other checks, and they might as well write one to you. We also accept MasterCard, Visa, and American Express credit card charges.

Sending the Return and Bill

The bill is prepared and generated by the tax preparation software. You should add to the bill the extra services not billed during the previous year. Many CPA firms bill clients based on time and complexity, taking into account the number of telephone calls from the client during the year. Follow-up billing is usually done, and late charges should be considered for past due accounts.

Our procedures are something like the following:

- Completed returns are given to the administrative assistant to copy and assemble.
- They are returned to the tax department to review the assembly.
- Part of this process is the reviewer actually looking at each page.
- He or she then puts on the "sign here" labels and makes sure a bill is included with the return.
- It is then given to the partner who will sign the return and perform a cursory review of it.
- That partner physically places the return in the mailing envelope and distributes the bills.
- The completed files are then given to tax control for entry and filing.

- A partner calls every client before the tax return is sent to give a heads-up on what to expect and that it is in line with advanced projections (or if not, why not).
- We do whatever possible to avoid having a client call us asking, "What do I do?" or "What happened?" The return is sent to the client with a copy of the return, a bill, the client's original information, and preaddressed envelopes to mail the returns. Note that e-filing will reduce and eliminate some of this process. We do not enclose separate letters of correspondence with the returns, except for a short personal memo from the partner, such as, "Hope all is well. If you have any questions, please call."

Starting at the end of June, we make follow-up phone calls to the clients for additional services and work that should be done for them. Of course, if the service the client needs is time sensitive, we follow up much sooner.

Whatever we can do to facilitate working with us, we do. We put "sign here" labels every place the client has to sign (this also makes it easier for the partner signing the return). We provide a listing of the postage rates and put some clients' return addresses on the envelopes. If a tax return is sent to a client to file and they are either housebound or the deadline is close, we put stamps for correct postage on envelopes.

Our marketing person calls every client a couple of days after the client is expected to have received the computed tax return to make sure the client has received it and to see if there is anything else he or she needs us to do.

Note that no one in our office is permitted to give any information to a client about whether he or she will get a refund or have additional tax to pay. This information can only be given by a partner, and we only give out the information after the return is completely finished and ready to be sent out. Giving out information prematurely only causes trouble. If the client is told incorrect information, he or she loses confidence in the staff. If told correct information, the client may not be happy with it and will complain. Premature information also generates additional telephone calls to me and my partners, which wastes time and doesn't accomplish anything.

Sample Bill for a Tax Return and Additional Services

It is important to provide an itemization of additional services performed. This is especially true when a client is expecting to pay an amount similar to the prior year's amount or based on the range estimated before the assignment began.

Following is a sample invoice:

Sample Invoice for Tax Return Preparation

Each additional service is specifically listed and priced.

Services in connection with your 20XX individual income tax returns:

Preparation of tax returns	$X,XXX
Software charge	FF
Preparation of Form 1045 (net operating loss carryback)	Y,YYY
Calculation of stock basis	ZZZ
Financial planning services during the past year	CCC
Calculation of capital gain on sale of vacation home	DDD
Tax notice service	EEE
Total due	$H,HHH

E-File Appropriate Returns 15

For the most part electronic filing is standard and must be done. With that said, here are some reasons and benefits.

Electronic filing greatly reduces paper handling, mailing costs (both ours for sending the return to the client and the client's for sending it to the governments), and rushes to get things in the mail so they are received in time for the client to post.

Electronic filing also helps the CPA firm because

- it reduces handling in the office (assembling and mailing).
- a paperless system makes it easier to retrieve and review in the digital filing system.
- digital retrieval is easier to access and review when a client calls with a question.
- e-filing saves the client time mailing, going to the post office, and getting a certified mail receipt.
- e-filing provides proof of filing.
- e-filing reduces IRS data entry error.
- e-filing speeds up refunds (which reduces telephone calls clients make to CPA firms to say they did not get their refund and to ask the firms to follow up).

Many states force electronic filing for any preparer firm that prepares more than a minimum number of returns (varies from state to state).

Firm administrative procedures have to be established to keep track of the forms the clients have to sign and return to you. You are generally required to have signed authorization in your possession before you can "push the button." However, at the last minute of tax season, this might not be possible. You should establish a protocol to get the client's assent to file, such as an e-mail response or even a telephone okay. If a client calls in his or her consent, the person taking the call should print out the signature form and write in it that the client called. Doing so keeps the procedures and handling process uniform, which is very important considering the large number of returns that are e-filed the last few days of tax season. One way to avoid a last minute rush is to have someone follow up a few days after the returns are sent to the client to ensure that the forms come back quickly.

A firm policy needs to be established if not every return can be e-filed (for example, if the federal return and three state returns can be e-filed for a client but not a fourth state's return). We would suggest e-filing every return that can be e-filed and using paper returns for those returns that can't be e-filed. Some cases in which returns cannot be e-filed are as follows:

- Withholding is more than 50 percent of the taxable wages.
- Social Security numbers for the taxpayer or dependents are incorrect.
- A dependent has been claimed by someone else (for example, a child is claimed by an ex-spouse).

An electronic filing checklist for individual tax returns is presented in exhibit 15-1, "Electronic Filing Checklist."

Last Minute Procedures

When sending out returns close to the filing deadline, you will need to highlight and stress to your clients the importance of them e-mailing or faxing the signed 8879 e-file authorization forms. If the clients put the forms in the mail, they may not be received in time for the deadline. Make sure the instructions for each return include your fax number, and then highlight the number before you send the return to the client.

EXHIBIT 15-1 **Electronic Filing Checklist—Procedures for Preparing Form 1040 for E-Filing**

The Process:

When e-filing returns, they will be prepared in the normal manner, making sure to complete the necessary e-filing requirements for each input sheet, and then tested for e-filing capabilities. If the returns are able to be e-filed, the client's copy of the returns will be sent to the client for approval, with either Form 8879, "IRS e-file Signature Authorization," if no attachments are required, or Form 8453, "U.S. Individual Income Tax Transmittal for an IRS e-file Return," with required attachments. The client will approve the returns for e-filing by having both spouses sign and return Forms 8879 or 8453 to us. Once the approved forms are received from the client, the returns can be e-filed. If the client is sent Form 8453, the original Form 8453 must be forwarded to the IRS within three business days after the e-filed return was accepted by the IRS. If the client signed Form 8879, this form will be kept in our files and will not be forwarded to the IRS. **If a New Jersey NJ-1040 or New York IT-201 is not going to be e-filed, a signed New Jersey Form NJ-1040-O or signed New York Form IT-800 must be obtained from the client. These forms are also to be kept in our files.**

Preparer Steps:

1. Prepare the return in the normal manner, making sure to complete the necessary e-filing requirements on each input sheet. Clear as many of the diagnostics as possible by clicking "View" on the tool bar and selecting "Diagnostics."
2. Once the return has been completed, it is now ready for the e-filing process.
3. Select "Electronic Filing" from the Organizer tree, and open "1040 Returns."

4. **Step 1:** Enable Electronic Filing. Our Electronic Filing Identification Number (EFIN) has been entered as a default setting:
    a. Check the "Enable Federal Filing" box.
    b. Check "Enable All Resident States" box or select individual states for filing.
5. **Step 2:** Personal Identification Numbers (PINs). We will be using the "Practitioner PIN" program; therefore, the "Practitioner PIN" box should be checked. Select the box to "Randomly generate the taxpayer and spouse PIN numbers."
    a. The Electronic Return Originator (ERO) PIN should be entered.
    b. This five-digit number is the signer's three- or four-digit employee number followed by one or two zeros. For example, if the signer is employee number 999, the ERO PIN would be 99900.
    c. Enter the date that the PINs were entered.
    d. If the return cannot be e-filed using the electronic signature method of Form 8879, it must be e-filed using the manual signature method of Form 8453.
    e. The manual method (Form 8453) must be used if there are special IRS forms, such as Form 8283, "Noncash Charitable Contributions"; Form 1098C, "Contributions of Motor Vehicles, Boats, and Airplanes"; or other paper attachments, such as schedules of capital gain transactions that are not entered on Fast Tax (see the list in the Fast Tax input sheet by clicking "Form 8453 Requirements and Selections").
6. **Step 3:** Direct Deposit or Debit. If the client wants to have his or her refund direct deposited or his or her account debited for payment, enter the information on the "Taxpayer Information" screen; it will

automatically carry to this screen. If the account is to be debited and the client does not give you a specific date to debit the account, use April 14 as a default date.

7. **Step 4:** Additional Information. Review the specific input for completeness. Do not override ERO and paid preparer information.
8. **Step 5:** Review Electronic Filing Diagnostics. Fully recompute the return. Follow the directions on this screen before you "Create Electronic File."
9. **Step 6:** Create Electronic File. Check the "Enable Federal Electronic Filing for this Return" box. Check the state return box(es), as needed. Finally, click "Create Electronic File for 1040 Returns."
   a. Note that any time a change is made to a return, you must recompute the return, clear the e-file diagnostics, and create a new electronic file.
   b. Once an electronic file is created, the return is "Qualified" for electronic filing. The return is now ready to print and give to the reviewer.
10. Processing the Return to Send to the Client. After the reviewer has completed his or her review, the return **must** be recomputed and a new "Electronic File" **must** be created. The return is then printed in final form, together with Forms 8879 or 8453, and given to Tax Processing for assembly. The return is assembled and given back to the reviewer to check the assembled return for completeness. Once completed, the return is given to the signer for signature and mailing to the client.

The reviewer's final step is to lock the return by entering the "Completed Date.

Process Extensions 16

When we prepare extensions, we do so using the tax preparation software. It prints the forms, as well as the instructions. We also prepare estimated taxes for all four quarters for the year. We know these amounts will change, but it is very unlikely that many returns will get done by June 15, so preparing the estimates for that date eliminates touching the client's file and reacclimating ourselves with the client's situation. If, by chance, the return is not done by September 15, we already gave the client that form, so the payment can be made. Also, by giving the client the estimates for the balance of the year, the client is aware of the approximate amounts he or she will need to pay. This helps the client in his or her cash flow planning.

We include the extension payment with the first quarter's estimated tax payment so that the client only has to write one check, and in case the extension payment was supposed to be greater than we estimated, the client's penalty and interest will be much lower if the client only has to pay the underpayment of estimated tax penalty for the first quarter. We can mitigate the penalty by preparing the return sooner.

We usually give the client a copy of the worksheet we used to estimate the April 15 tax payment.

Extensions are necessary when the following are true:

1. The client did not receive some K-1s or 1099s or other documents with information that you need to report.
2. The client did not receive letters confirming charitable contributions that are required to be in your possession by the due date of your tax return.
3. There is pending litigation or a tax audit and reporting certain transactions might prejudice your position or you are awaiting resolution which might affect an item on this year's return.
4. The client might want to reverse a prior year IRA conversion to a Roth IRA and would rather not file by April 15 so an amended

return would not be necessary if you decide to reverse the conversion by October 15, 20XX.

5. Circumstances may have prohibited the client from assembling all your information properly. This might also include searching for tax basis of securities or assets that have been sold.
6. Client has a complicated situation and it is best to have an extension so the preparer would have more time to devote to the return.
7. Client might want to open or fund a SEP pension plan; client may also want to open and fund such a plan. By extending, you will have until October 15 to make your decision. If you have a Keogh, 401(k), or SIMPLE plan, the contribution for last year can be made by the extended due date, but the Keogh and 401(k) must have been established by the previous December 31 and the SIMPLE by September 30 of the tax year (crazy and inconsistent rules for basically the same type of deductions).
8. Client did not file last year's return and feels that filing this year's return before the prior year will cause extra IRS attention. However, irrespective of what client did not file, he or she should file this year's return on time which would be the extended due date.
9. Those with an installment sale might want to wait as long as possible to file while they consider electing out of the installment sale if their prior year taxable income is expected to be substantially lower than 2014.
10. People with net operating or other losses that can be carried back might want to delay filing to determine if they should elect to forego that and carry it forward.
11. The extension can delay elections that are made on the first-filed tax return reporting certain new transactions.
12. The extension is for a gift tax return where not all the issues are clear including generation skipping elections and spousal consents, or where basis information is not readily available or discount valuations are not completed.
13. There is a high risk of audit; filing an extension might reduce the chance of an audit. Note that it will not lower the chance of a computer-generated notice questioning an item or picking up income that was not reported.

14. If the tax preparer is unable to devote the necessary time to get the return ready to file on time.
15. An error is discovered on a prior year's return and additional time is needed to research and correct it, and the current year's return might be affected by the change.

Comment: The extension is to delay the filing, not the payment. Payments must be timely made. Also, do not forget to also file a state extension if applicable.

Letter to Explain Extension to a Client

Dear________________________,

As you are aware, we will be filing an extension for your 20XX income tax return.

The extension will permit you to file your return after April 15 (this year's due date) but will not permit late payment of your taxes beyond that date. In order to properly estimate your balance due, if any for 20XX, we will need an estimate of your gross 20XX income and expenses. If the income and expenses are consistent with 20WW, or with a 20XX projection we previously prepared for you, let us know and we will estimate your tax liability based on that. At a minimum, we will need copies of your W-2 forms, 1099-R, and any other forms indicating withholding taxes and a listing of the estimated tax payments you made and the dates and payees. See checklist attached.

If you will not owe any money, we will take care of all the paperwork and filing and you will not have to do anything. If you owe taxes, we will either send you the forms or you can download them from our secure portal. To keep your personal information secure, we will not email you the forms.

When your tax return is completed, you will be fully credited with the payments made with the extensions.

We will prepare your 20YY estimated tax vouchers based on the projected tax for 20XX. When your 20XX tax return is finally prepared, we will make any necessary changes for your remaining estimated tax payments.

For ease of filing, and to potentially reduce overall penalties should the projections of your 20XX tax be less than the tax when your return is finalized, we will be combining the projected amount due for 20XX with your first quarter 20YY estimated tax payment. The combined amount will cover you for both taxes, but if there is an under payment, the payment will be first applied to the 20XX tax liability and any remainder to your 20YY estimated tax.

The extensions will be for your federal and state returns and the final due date will be October 15, 20YY. However, please send us your full tax information as soon as you have it assembled. It will be best to not wait until the last minute.

If any questions, don't hesitate to call me.

Cordially,

[Accountant Name]

Letter to Explain Extension to a Client—Accountant Workload

Use same letter, but make sure you call client to explain why you need to file the extension. Tell client you will pay any penalties but there shouldn't be any if the client pays the tax amount you tell them to. Do not put in any letter or email the reason why you cannot complete the return on time.

Checklist of Needed Information to Prepare Extension

Must haves:

___W-2 forms

___1099-R forms

___Listing of all 20XX estimated tax payments (including payments made by January 15, 20YY)

___Any other forms you received with withholding tax

___Estimates of other income you received

___Estimates of your deductions

___Any government notices you received changing your 20WW tax or 20XX estimated taxes (or both)

Optional:

___Summary of capital gains transactions

___1099s for interest, dividends and security transactions

___1099-MISC you may have received

___K-1s for pass through entities such as Partnerships, LLCs, S Corporations, Trusts, Estates

___Form 1098 Mortgage payment statements

___Form 1099-C for cancellation of indebtedness

___A balance sheet and profit and loss statement for any self-employed activity or business

___Anything you think would be helpful in determining your projected 20XX taxable income

___All of your tax information that we will need to prepare your return

Letter to Accompany Extension Payment Worksheet

Dear ________________________,

Attached is a worksheet calculating your extension payment and if applicable your 20YY first quarter estimated tax payment.

Based on information you provided, we estimated your 20XX tax, gave you credit for your withholdings and estimated tax payments, and arrived at a balance due. Additionally, we used that information to calculate your 20YY estimated tax payments, and included the first quarter payment with the balance due for 20XX.

We also enclosed estimated tax vouchers that need to be paid June 15, September 15 and either by December 31, 20XX, or January 15, 20YY. These amounts will be adjusted when your 20XX tax return is completed, and you will receive replacement forms for remaining payments.

These amounts are based on the information you provided and most likely will change when your tax return is actually completed.

For ease of filing, and to potentially reduce overall penalties should the projections of your 20XX tax be less than the actually determined tax when your return is finalized, we combined the projected amount due for 20XX with your first quarter 20YY estimated tax payment. The combined amount will cover you for both taxes, but if there is an under payment, the payment will be first applied to the 20XX tax liability and any remainder to your 20YY estimated tax. Therefore, only one check is necessary for the two tax payments.

The extensions will be for your federal and state returns and the final due date will be October 15, 20YY.

If any questions, don't hesitate to call me.

Cordially,

[Accountant Name]

Following is a worksheet that can be used to calculate the extension amounts and payments to be made:

Sample Extension Worksheet

Client ______________________________

20WW extension tax payments and 20XX estimated tax

Date prepared __________ **by** ________

	Federal	State ____	State ____	State ____	Other ____
Projected 20WW tax					
Payments:					
Withholding					
Withholding					
Overpayment from 20VV					
4/15/WW est. tax paid					
6/15/WW est. tax paid					
9/15/WW est. tax paid					
12/31/WW est. tax paid					
1/15/XX est. tax paid					

Total payments					
Total due (overpmt) for 20WW					
Estimated 20XX tax					
Estimated withholding					
Estimated tax to be paid					
1st Qtr. 20XX est. payment					
Total income tax to be pd.					
20WW Gift tax – Taxpayer					
20WW Gift tax – Spouse					
Total to be paid 4/15/XX					

Assist with Tax Audits 17

Tax audits are always a possibility, and we bill extra for audits. Some of the various types of audits and activities are as follows:

- Office audits.
- Field examinations.
- Audits of pension plans and nonprofit organizations.
- Preparation of appeals and protests.
- Tax court petitions. CPAs can be admitted to practice before the United States Tax Court if they show a need to be admitted and pass a biannual test. Being admitted to practice will enable you to file tax court petitions, which will give you at least two additional chances for negotiation and settling a case. The tests are given once every other year, usually in September, October, or November in Washington, D.C. Fewer than 200 nonattorneys are admitted. For the exact date and location of the next exam, go to the United States Tax Court website at www.USTaxCourt.gov and click on "Forms" and "Admission Information for Nonattorneys." You can call the United States Tax Court at 1-202-521-0700 or write to them at 400 Second Street, NW, Washington, DC 20217. You can also purchase copies of previous exams and the rules of procedure. Note that I am admitted to practice and have tried cases in Tax Court. If you are interested in becoming admitted and want to discuss, you are welcome to contact me at emendlowitz@withum.com.
- Criminal tax cases, including liaison with counsel.
- State tax audits and appeals, including sales, income, and personal property taxes and penalties.

The tax department, specifically an audit specialist, usually handles the audit, not the preparer or engagement partner. Other tips for assisting with a tax audit include the following:

- The practitioner must adequately prepare for the audit. Note that the amount of preparation time is inversely proportional to the time spent with the agent.
- The CPA must be skilled in negotiating strategies.
- The CPA must know when to be quiet and listen.

The accountant must be able to handle sensitive matters, including underreporting of income and other potential criminal acts, and must know when to insist that something be reported, as well as how to walk away from the engagement. Accountants must always be cognizant that they risk their license, livelihood, and liberty when they engage in illegal actions or look away from a client engaging in those actions. Accountants must always be aware of their legal, ethical, and moral responsibilities. CPAs should do nothing that they cannot clearly defend and explain should they be on a witness stand, and they should assume that they might be in that position for everything they do.

There are two ways to be engaged by a client to represent him or her during an audit. The first method is when the client receives a notice and contacts the firm for help. Exhibit 17-1, "Sample Tax Audit Engagement Letter," is a template that can be used for a client's tax examination.

Additionally, some accounting firms are offering an audit insurance or protection plan under which the accountant's fee is covered by the initial payment made under the plan. Exhibit 17-2, "Sample Audit Protection Service Letter and Bill," is a letter and the accompanying bill for such service. This plan is offered to most of the low-risk clients for a nominal fee.

EXHIBIT 17-1 Sample Tax Audit Engagement Letter

[*Date*]

[*Client Name*]
[*Client Address*]

Dear [*Client Name*],

This letter will confirm the arrangements for our representation with respect to Internal Revenue Service's examination of your individual income tax return for the years 20WW and 20XX.

Tax Audit Services

We will represent you before the Internal Revenue Service during this examination, unless the arrangement is terminated in writing by either party. Furthermore, in the event we cannot resolve all of the issues at the initial level, we will be available to appeal any proposed deficiencies or penalties at the Appeals Division of the Internal Revenue Service, although that appeal is not part of this engagement.

We will not audit, or otherwise verify, any information provided by you for presentation to the Internal Revenue Service during the course of the examination, unless we deem it necessary or you specifically request us to do so in writing. However, we may ask you for further clarification, and we expect you to provide that clarification promptly and candidly.

Our communications are confidential, not privileged. That is, they may not be disclosed unless you approve under most circumstances. On the other hand, privileged communications are not permitted to be disclosed, even in court. Although there is now a limited CPA-client privilege in federal matters, it does not apply to matters prior to the passage of the Internal Revenue Service Restructuring and Reform Act of 1998 and does not apply to state matters. Accordingly, if we are served by a properly issued administrative summons compelling us to testify in court proceedings, even our confidential communications could be subject to disclosure.

The tax agencies have recently begun emphasizing a number of procedures during examinations to ascertain that taxpayers have complied with their tax filing responsibilities. These procedures have led to a growing number of requests by examining agents to interview the taxpayer directly. However, you do have a statutory right to be represented and not to meet with the examining agent (unless you are served with an enforceable administrative summons). It is in your best interest to refer any questions or other contact from the agent to us without discussing the case with the agent. By signing this engagement letter, you acknowledge that any direct contact by the Internal Revenue Service will be promptly referred to us as your authorized representative. It is hereby acknowledged that if you choose to appear before, or discuss this case with, the agent against our advice, you do so at your own risk.

Fees

Fees and expenses are due and payable upon presentation of our invoice to you. Our fee for representing you will be based upon our time, billed at our rate of $XXX per hour for partners and $XX–$XXX per hour for staff, plus out-of-pocket expenses. We anticipate that most of the services involved in the exam will be performed by a partner. In order to proceed, we require a retainer in the amount of $XXXX.

If we have not received payment in accordance with the stated terms, we reserve the right to terminate this engagement with no further notice.

Conclusion

If this letter reflects your understanding of the terms of our engagement, please sign below and return one copy to us with the retainer amount.

We want to express our appreciation for this opportunity to serve you.

Sincerely,

[***Partner Signature***]

Accepted by:

Client's signature:

Date:

Note that most Professional Malpractice Insurance Carriers have recommended draft engagement letters and it is recommended that you use them as a resource.

EXHIBIT 17-2 Sample Audit Protection Service Letter and Bill

April 2, 20XX

[*Client Name*]
[*Client Address*]

Re: Audit Protection Service

Dear [*Client Name*],

This letter concerns a method we have initiated in order to limit our fees in the eventuality of your being audited by the IRS. We call this our audit protection service.

For the additional fee of this audit protection service, we will represent you at the IRS and the applicable resident state tax authority for a field or office audit on your 20YY tax return, and respond to any and all of the preceding tax authority inquiries on your 20YY return, without additional charge to you. This service does not cover appeals. This service will be performed at any time that your 20YY tax return is audited or questioned, which may be as late as 20ZZ. Our normal fee for this service is based on our hourly rate schedule and would greatly exceed the cost of this protection plan. As you are aware, we cannot guarantee that there will be no tax changes, interest, or penalties, but we will represent you and act for your best interests at no additional fee.

An income tax audit is a time-consuming ordeal that requires work by the taxpayer to gather the evidential information, as well as a professional to prepare and represent the taxpayer's case before the authorities. In general, our charges for this service usually run in excess of the fee for preparing the tax return.

We are offering you this audit protection for the nominal charge of $XXX. This offer will expire 30 days from the date of this letter.

If you agree to our firm providing this service for you, please acknowledge such by signing and dating below and paying the total amount due, including audit protection, on the enclosed bill. We will then forward you a power of attorney form for your signature. This will enable the IRS to forward us copies of all correspondence regarding your 20YY return. We will also, with your approval, check a box on your tax return that will grant permission for the taxing authorities to speak and deal with us on any matter arising from the filed return.

Should you elect not to subscribe to the audit protection, simply pay the total without audit protection amount on the enclosed bill. This letter and the enclosed bill will be the only correspondence we will send you relating to audit protection.

If you have any questions, please feel free to call us.

Cordially,

[*Partner Signature*]

Acknowledged:

Signature:

Date:

Bill Accompanying the Audit Protection Letter

Preparation of 20YY federal and state individual income tax returns should be charged as follows:

Tax preparation fee	$XXX.xx
Optional audit protection service (see the enclosed letter.)	YYY.yy
Total with audit protection	$ZZZ.zz

Note that the audit insurance is an additional charge of between 15 percent and 25 percent of the preparation of the fee that is paid when the tax return is prepared and will cover the CPA's fee for handling the audit. It does not cover penalties and interest.

In addition to the audit insurance, we started charging every client a tax notice fee that we added to his or her tax preparation fee to cover our charges for responding to tax agency notices. Approximately 75 percent of our clients paid it. We used lower amounts than for the audit insurance and did not charge clients for both protection services.

SECTION III

Client Satisfaction, Retention, and Referrals: Measure of Tax Return Client Satisfaction 18

What Clients Get Is Part of Your Brand

We continually give clients "things." They get tax returns, financial statements, newsletters, notes, e-mails, memos, and a myriad of other things. How these things are presented or delivered establishes your brand. Some firms place client copies of tax returns in binders with fancy covers, but others staple them sloppily and throw them in an envelope messily addressed to the client. Every contact creates an image and affects the way you are perceived.

An overly professional image is not always the appropriate way to proceed, but a sloppy image is always inappropriate.

You can be perceived as sloppy in differing ways. Everything can be done in the most professional, high-class manner, but the envelope could be addressed to a "Mr." when the client is a "Dr." Sloppy! The postage meter indicia could be faint, needing ink. Sloppy! The envelope could be addressed to a former address. Sloppy! Insufficient postage could be placed on the envelope. Sloppy! You could deliver the tax return to the client at the last minute to be mailed and not put stamps on the attached envelopes for the returns to be sent to the tax authorities. Sloppy! Sending your monthly e-newsletter on the last couple of days in the month. Sloppy!

Actually, not being state of the art, such as accepting digital organizers, can be perceived as sloppy or, minimally, not current.

When you deliver something to a client, it serves the utility of giving the client what he or she paid for. However, it also serves a promotional or marketing purpose.

Many firms now have online portals in which a client can log on and access his or her files and download his or her returns. This is a more secure way of doing things than e-mail. At some point, this will become a standard procedure. Isn't it better to start with it now, rather than being one of the last to adopt this procedure?

Another way to send, receive, and retrieve files is to use secure file transfer services. They are easy to use, and you do not need a portal. They are much better than e-mail for security and are priced quite reasonably. Using them could make you out as being fully state of the art.

Quality Control Client Survey

Some firms include a client survey report asking for an evaluation of the firm's services. These forms are included with every tax return and financial statement that is sent to a client, sent after tax season ends, or at a predetermined calendar date such as June 30 or November 1 Sections are divided into categories that ask clients to evaluate and comment on timeliness, the understanding of the client's business and industry, staff responsiveness, the value of the services provided to the client, and what the firm could do to better serve the client, along with suggestions about recommending the firm to others.

To be fully effective, all client concerns and comments should be followed up with the client and with a review of the firm's systemic issues. This form can be used as part of a continuous improvement program.

Cover Letter With Client Quality Survey

Date

Address

Dear:

We recently completed services for ___________. As part of our continued commitment to excellence, we would appreciate your taking a few minutes to tell us how we did and how we can improve.

We are constantly trying to enhance the value of our services to our clients. Your comments are very important to us in achieving that objective. Please complete the attached questionnaire and return it to me in the enclosed envelope or contact me on my direct line at 1-XXX-XXX-XXXX.

Thank you for taking the time to assist us. We assure you that your input will be used to help us provide the highest value service possible.

Sincerely,

Name goes here, CPA

Partner

Top 10 Reasons Why a Client Should Use You

If you cannot think of 10 reasons, how about 5? What about 2?

10:

9:

8:

7:

6:

5:

4:

3:

2:

1:

If you want some good reasons, look at your clients' answers to the survey questions and make sure they are all "5s."

Some other reasons:

- We really care about our clients. (Do your clients know that?) Does everything you do lead to that thought?
- We continuously keep in touch with our clients. Do you?
- When we work on your return, we aren't filling out a form; we are focusing on ways to help you save money, create wealth, and be more secure in your finances. Does everyone at your firm live and breathe this?
- Our organization has the experience to apply our broad knowledge to help our clients. Is there collaboration between various experts or specialists to consider each client's situation?
- Partners look at every tax return before it is finalized. You better make sure this is so!

Please assist us to better serve you by responding to this survey.

Please rate your satisfaction with the tax returns prepared by the firm on a scale of 1 to 5, with 5 being highly satisfied and 1 being not satisfied.

	Satisfaction Rating High — Low					
	5	4	3	2	1	
TIMELINESS						
We completed your project within the expected timeframe.	5	4	3	2	1	N/A
We met promised dates throughout the process.	5	4	3	2	1	N/A
We returned phone calls promptly.	5	4	3	2	1	N/A
Our frequency of contact with you was adequate.	5	4	3	2	1	N/A
We informed you if there would be any kind of delay.	5	4	3	2	1	N/A
Our staff kept you informed of our progress.	5	4	3	2	1	N/A
KNOWING YOUR BUSINESS AND INDUSTRY						
Our staff was proficient in their technical area of expertise.	5	4	3	2	1	N/A
Our staff offered valuable suggestions.	5	4	3	2	1	N/A
Our staff was up to date and informed on business issues affecting you.	5	4	3	2	1	N/A

(continued)

OUR PEOPLE						
Our staff were available when you needed them.	5	4	3	2	1	N/A
Our staff took an active interest in your business.	5	4	3	2	1	N/A
Our staff were responsive to your needs.	5	4	3	2	1	N/A
Our staff were friendly and courteous.	5	4	3	2	1	N/A
Our staff followed up on open items.	5	4	3	2	1	N/A
Our staff looked for extra ways to be helpful.	5	4	3	2	1	N/A
Our staff looked for ways to help you improve your profitability.	5	4	3	2	1	N/A
Our staff were professional in appearance and conduct.	5	4	3	2	1	N/A
Our staff worked well with your people with minimal disruptions.	5	4	3	2	1	N/A
TOTAL FIRM VALUE						
Overall performance of our staff.	5	4	3	2	1	N/A
Overall timeliness of our delivery to you.	5	4	3	2	1	N/A
Overall appearance of our reports.	5	4	3	2	1	N/A
Overall quality of our work.	5	4	3	2	1	N/A
Value received for fees billed.	5	4	3	2	1	N/A

(PLEASE USE THE BACK OF THIS SHEET IF MORE SPACE IS NEEDED)

CONTINUATION SHEET FOR ADDITIONAL COMMENTS

What could we have changed to improve our service?______

____

____

What did you like the most about our service? ___________

____

____

What is the most important function that we serve for you?

____

____

Are we performing that function to your complete satisfaction?
( ) Yes ( ) No Please explain. ____________________

____

____

Is there something exemplary that you would say about our firm or specific individuals in the firm? ______________

____

____

During the past year, did we cause you any surprises, problems, or disappointments? Please explain. __________

____

____

Did the services we provide meet or exceed your expectations?
( ) Yes ( ) No Please explain. ____________________

____

____

(continued)

Have you recommended our firm to others? ( ) Yes ( ) No

Would you recommend our firm if you had the opportunity to do so? ( ) Yes ( ) No Please explain.____________________

Are there services that you feel we should be offering that we don't? ( ) Yes ( ) No Please explain. ____________________

Any other comments: ____________________

Your Name and Title:____________________

Name of Business or Organization:____________________

Address: ____________________

Thank you for responding to this survey. We greatly appreciate your input. Please mail the completed survey in the enclosed return address envelope or scan and e-mail it to managingpartner@emailaddress.com.

How would your work score on this survey?

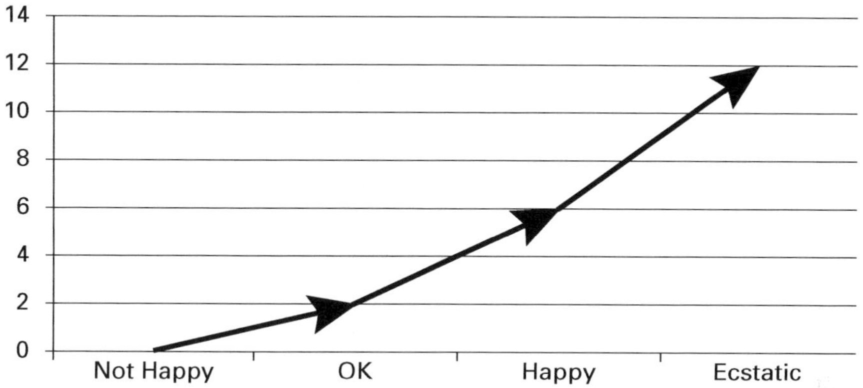

A measure of your clients' satisfaction is the number of referrals you get per year. The preceding chart indicates that the greater the satisfaction, the greater the referrals you can expect.

It has been my experience that newer clients tend to refer more than long-term clients. One reason is their excitement in deciding to get a new accountant and their confirmation of that excitement by recommending their friends also switch. Long-term clients have either referred all their acquaintances or *think* they have, so they generate fewer referrals. Also, the excitement has worn out. The point is that you should work to create excitement and never forget to WOW! your clients.

WOW! Your Clients

We tried many different ways to WOW! clients. Not everything worked but some did, and those successes make the efforts worthwhile.

A WOW! is something you do to make your clients say "WOW!" Some of these are things you can say at the tax return interview meeting, but these have low payback because they are forgotten until the next year's meeting or simply are not remembered clearly to compel any action.

I have found it effective to make follow-up calls starting in mid-May and running until close to the tax projection season in late October. Then, the tax preparation calls start. These calls can be very brief reminders about some things we spoke about and can lead to additional assignments, with clients coming into the office for meetings and discussions.

Keeping in Touch With Clients

Client surveys are a good way to keep in touch with clients and obtain assessments of how you did. Another way is to send your clients a post-tax season letter thanking them and letting them know how much you appreciate their confidence in you. Following are two letters you can consider. It is also a subtle way to let them know you perform other services—look at the P.S. in the first letter. That is a technique I like to use. The second letter can be adapted, but here it is used to send to clients of an acquired practice. It mentions in the body additional services you perform.

POST TAX SEASON LETTER TO CLIENTS—Version 1

Dear Client,

Tax season is certainly the busiest time for accounting firms, as was this year's tax season but it was extremely successful because of clients like you, and we thank you.

Tax preparation is an intricate process. Information is received—by postal mail, email or by personal meetings, an administrative person logs in the receipt and sets up our internal tracking so we can chart the progress of your return, documents are sorted and scanned, occasionally information is downloaded and populated into our tax programs, a preparer works on the return, a skilled experienced reviewer checks it over and also looks for tax savings and planning opportunities, then I look it over, adding my experience and understanding of your situation, ultimately approving and signing off on it. Our admin person then assembles the return, sends it to you and files it in our paperless cloud-based secure system. If you are e-filing, we await receipt of your signed approval and then we "push the button" and track the return until we receive notification it was properly filed. And in spite of all these steps, your return was given careful thoughtful and deliberate attention, your privacy was not compromised, your documents were not misplaced and you did your duty as a responsible citizen.

We thank you for your cooperation, understanding, and business. We appreciate what you mean to us.

Thank you.

Cordially,

Partner

P.S. Tax season is not our only business. We are open the rest of the year and are available to assist you in financial planning, estate planning, goal setting, assistance with how you should invest your IRA, 401(k), 403b funds, and help with starting or buying a business. We are here for you with anything financial that might concern you. Give us a call to discuss how we can add value and make your life easier.

POST TAX SEASON LETTER TO CLIENTS—Version 2

Dear Client:

The 20XX tax season is finally over! And while it's never too early to start planning for 20YY, and all those tax changes, we want to first thank you for allowing us to be of service and being part of what we hope continues to be a successful long-term relationship.

It's hard to believe that it's been three years since we acquired Jim's practice. The gradual client transition has gone very well. For those of you who we have had the pleasure of working with, we hope you've been pleased. We look forward to eventually working with every one of you.

We also hope you liked the new office. Everyone appreciated the easier parking and accessibility. We all have a little more room and privacy now. And yes, we miss the dog too!

As many of you know, tax preparation is not our only business. We are here year-round providing accounting and payroll services to many small and mid-sized businesses. Thinking of starting a business? We can help with that also.

In addition, we also offer personal financial planning services. This could range from advice on starting a college savings plan or rolling over a 401(k) to a comprehensive financial evaluation and plan. To give you an idea of how working with a financial planner could benefit you, I'm offering a complimentary portfolio and beneficiary review. Please call or email me for details and to set up your appointment.

Our goal is to provide you with a superior tax and business service. To do that, we're constantly looking for ways to improve and innovate. If you have any comments or suggestions, please let us know. We look forward to your feedback.

We want to again thank you for trusting your important tax and financial matters to us. We certainly value that relationship. Because we do not advertise, we accept new clients by referral only. If you know people who might benefit from our expertise, please give them one of our business cards. Otherwise, we look forward to seeing you next year or sooner, if you have one of those situations where you need to talk to your "tax adviser." That would be us!

Cordially,

How Did You Do?

Tax season is by far the busiest time year for accountants. Many are glad it's over and don't like to look back. However, I have found a thorough assessment early on after tax season ends is a good way to find ways to improve processes, training, review, and client service. Here is a checklist you can consider using.

POST TAX SEASON ASSESSMENT CHECKLIST

Overall Procedures

- ☐ Assess the effectiveness of coordination between tax preparation and regular work.
- ☐ Discuss the success and options for managing seasonality.
- ☐ Consider ways client relations could be improved or strengthened.
- ☐ Was turnaround time acceptable?
- ☐ Could the quality of deliverables be improved or made more user-friendly?
- ☐ How was the effectiveness of staff training?
- ☐ How did total staff hours compare to last year and was it adequate or excessive?
- ☐ Evaluate methods of staff tax season compensation.
- ☐ Weigh the growth of individual staff and whether any "stars" developed.
- ☐ What was the degree and success of peer interaction?
- ☐ How effective was intra-firm communications.
- ☐ How well was the integration of new staff and clients into the practice?
- ☐ How did the quality and quantity of client comments compare to past tax seasons?
- ☐ Determine profitability and cash flow from tax season work.

Meetings with clients to get information

- ☐ Was information put into process within one day of meeting?
- ☐ If information was not complete, how long afterwards was it put into process?
- ☐ Were information follow-up questions properly noted with a follow-up date and responsible party?

- ☐ If client's questions needed immediate follow up, how quickly was it done?
- ☐ Was client's experience in our office pleasant?
  - Did we keep client waiting?
  - Was client offered something to drink?
  - Did the meeting last more than15 minutes longer than scheduled?
- ☐ Did clients come prepared with neatly organized data and completed organizer?
- ☐ Did many clients "waste" our time by opening mail and sorting data that should have been done before meeting?

Information received by mail or email

- ☐ Was the client informed it was received?
- ☐ Was the client given a contact person or name of preparer?
- ☐ Was an approximate or outside completion date furnished?
- ☐ Were client's special instructions followed?
- ☐ Were client's questions to partner addressed?

Preparation

- ☐ Was the return data entered in the smart scanner?
- ☐ Were the documents bookmarked?
- ☐ Were the preparers properly trained based level of complexity of returns they were assigned?
- ☐ What changes in training methods are suggested?
- ☐ If research was needed, did preparer perform initial research in one volume tax handbook or online? Was answer found or did preparer neglect to do initial research?
- ☐ When research was assigned, was the question or issue clearly stated along with a time budget and contact person for the reply?

- ☐ Did the preparer have a "go-to" or resource person to answer questions (either technical, procedural or client specific)?
- ☐ Did preparer familiarize himself or herself with planning done during the year?
- ☐ Did preparer review and compare final results of the return to previous year?
- ☐ Was return submitted to review within one week of being assigned to preparer?

Review

- ☐ Was review time reasonable (less than 25 percent of preparer time)?
- ☐ Were review comments excessive based on complexity of return?
- ☐ Was return reassigned to preparer or did reviewer or someone else make corrections?
- ☐ Was return resubmitted to reviewer within two days of being assigned to make corrections?
- ☐ Did preparer complete all necessary checklists and worksheets?
- ☐ Were review comments and diagnostics addressed completely?
- ☐ Were the reviewers properly trained?
- ☐ If non-tax managers or partners reviewed returns, did they do a satisfactory job?
- ☐ Were there any bottlenecks with the review or with a reviewer that were not cleared up within one day?
- ☐ Were there delays in needed decisions from partners or managers?
- ☐ Were review notes evaluated in the aggregate after tax season to uncover repetitive errors?
- ☐ Were follow up notes for the current year filed properly for easy retrieval next year?

Administrative

☐ Was information receipt entered in the tax control and flow software within one day?

☐ When entered, was it assigned to a preparer?

☐ Was the turnaround from the administrative staff satisfactory?

☐ Were administrative personnel properly trained and oriented to tax season?

☐ Did admin people find preparation or procedural errors?

☐ What was admin staff reaction to "redos"?

☐ Was the final return placed in the paperless filing system when processed, or was there a delay?

☐ Did bills accompany the returns?

☐ Were there delays or difficulty in tracking returns?

☐ Did admin staff work adequate overtime or hours?

☐ If the firm has more than one administrative staff member, did they work staggered hours so someone was available whenever preparers and reviewers were working?

Staffing

☐ Were staff properly assigned?

☐ Did bottlenecks develop with any individual staff person?

☐ Were any staff apparently under- or overused?

☐ Did all staff perform roughly the same number of hours?

☐ What conclusions arise from a review of the hours and performance of the staff members with the highest and fewest tax season hours?

☐ Does a review of days off show any patterns of absences?

- ☐ Review and discuss the error rates for returns done throughout tax season. Were more errors detected at the beginning, middle, or end of the season?
- ☐ Should there have been additional staff hired for tax season?
- ☐ How did new staff or interns perform after their initial training?
- ☐ What worked or needed changing in staff scheduling procedures?
- ☐ Did too many people get involved in certain returns?
- ☐ Was there a reduction in time or quality on regular work?
- ☐ Are any preparers ready to become reviewers?
- ☐ Was there satisfactory growth and development of preparers?
- ☐ Was the staff excited about tax season and was that excitement conveyed to clients?
- ☐ Was any work outsourced other than the smart scanner?
- ☐ Was the quality of the outsourced work satisfactory?

Error Reduction

- ☐ What error patterns can be identified? How can they be categorized? (Don't concentrate on isolated instances.) What steps could reduce or eliminate them?
- ☐ Was every discovered error on a delivered return addressed immediately by a partner?
- ☐ Did specific staff members have higher error rates? What types of errors were involved? For instance, if an inexperienced staff person had high error rates because of inadequate instruction, then it may be the instructor, and not necessarily the preparer, who needs additional training.

- ☐ To what extent were errors caused by interruptions? What types of interruptions? (Examples: partner, peer, telephone or email, or missing information that should have been identified and obtained before the return was started.)
- ☐ To what extent would errors have been avoided had checklists been properly used or standard procedures followed?
- ☐ What types of tax notices did clients receive? Could they have been avoided with a change in procedures? (For example, if they were due to incorrect estimated tax payments reported on the return, the notice could have been avoided by requiring clients to furnish proof of their payments.)
- ☐ What kinds of errors did partners find when they received returns ready to be signed and mailed?
- ☐ What policy will the firm use to monitor and prevent errors going forward?

Client Communications

- ☐ Were clients called by a manager or partner with news of unexpected results (that is, refunds under or over expected amounts)?
- ☐ What kinds of client complaints were received? How were they handled and by whom?
- ☐ Were deliverables "user-friendly"? (That is, understandable and complete.)
- ☐ Did an administrative person call clients to ensure the return was received?
- ☐ Did clients have problems using the firm's secure portal?
- ☐ Will the partner keep in touch with tax preparation clients during the year?
- ☐ Was the period between information receipt and first contact for additional information reasonable (by client standards)?

- ☐ Was there frequent follow up (at least once every three days)?

Partner Interaction

- ☐ Did the partners receive too many phone calls or emails from clients with complaints?
- ☐ Did those contacts involve issues lower-level staff could have or should have addressed before the contact became necessary?
- ☐ Were there fee complaints?
- ☐ Did staff complain about partners' accessibility?
- ☐ Did partners turn around or sign off on returns within one day of receiving them?
- ☐ Were partners available to assess or close bottlenecks in the procedures?
- ☐ Did partners discover errors in returns that were ready for their final review and signature?
- ☐ Did partners detect a rushed or harried atmosphere among the staff?

Seasonality

- ☐ Were the overtime hours sufficient to complete all tax returns on time?
- ☐ Were more temporary tax season staff needed?
- ☐ Did the seasonal help get adequate in-house training and was their work satisfactory?
- ☐ If interns were used to prepare returns, was their work satisfactory? Did they have positive experiences at the firm? Should any be offered permanent positions?
- ☐ Could more work have been done by a client rather than the firm (such as capital gain transaction schedules, schedules of rental property income and expenses or write ups of schedule C transactions in small business accounting software)?

- ☐ Did individual returns get backlogged because of the firm's failure to timely prepare business returns that provided K-1s?
- ☐ Could some of the work on business returns have been done toward the end of last year or early in this year before the firm got busy with individual tax returns?

Extensions

- ☐ Were extensions encouraged or discouraged?
- ☐ Were extensions filed for returns when all the information to process them was available?
- ☐ Was the first quarter estimated tax combined with the extension amounts on the extension form?
- ☐ Were the remaining three quarters' estimated tax vouchers prepared and provided to clients with extensions even though the amounts might change when the return is eventually completed?

Billing

- ☐ Were bills delivered with every return sent to clients?
- ☐ Were billing amounts discussed with the partner before the bill was prepared?
- ☐ Were fees increased? If so, for what amounts and what percentage of the clients?
- ☐ Were additional or new services separately itemized on bills?

Additional Client Services and Marketing

- ☐ Were clients informed about available additional post-tax season services? If not, why not? Which firm members did or did not identify additional service options?
- ☐ Were additional services a client needed documented in a follow-up file?

- ☐ How many new tax clients were obtained? What were the sources?
- ☐ What was the average fee of the new clients?
- ☐ If some tax clients did not return, what were the reasons?
- ☐ What follow-up procedures will be used to explain the need for—and availability of—additional services?
- ☐ How well did the firm do in actually performing additional services that were identified during last tax season?
- ☐ Were client surveys sent with the returns? If not, they should be sent now. Survey responses should be reviewed for patterns and with a focus on unfavorable responses.
- ☐ The assessment should also identify clients that will need current year pre-year-end planning, tax projections, and additional services.

Client Loyalty and Responsibility

Client loyalty is what keeps a client returning to you each year. You might believe it is your superior work or service or low fees, but it is loyalty. The loyalty might be fueled by your superior work or service and reasonable fees, but retention still comes down to loyalty. It might also be fueled by your location and availability, but it is still their loyalty.

Now, let me ask you a question. Do you return that loyalty? If the loyalty is one-sided, and I believe it usually is felt more strongly by the customer than the vendor, then at some point, there will be a crack in the loyalty shield, and loyalty will disintegrate quite quickly.

To avoid taking your clients for granted, try the following. Put yourself in your clients' position and review the questions in the sample client quality surveys.

Also, try to take a lesson from social media and create a community among your clients. Try surprising your clients with personal notes or copies of articles, phone calls, newsletters, and even a surprise gift of a book or something related to their hobbies, interests, businesses, or professions. Everyone likes to receive something for free. Try sending a book with each individual tax return sent to a client or when you return their information or in a separate package. Remember how good you feel when you receive an extra bag of peanuts on an airplane (when they used to do this—I think they now charge $9.25 for each bag of peanuts)!

Here is a word about client responsibilities and how clients can keep fees down and not delay turnaround time.

Responsiveness is very important from the professionals a client engages, but it is equally important for the client to return that responsiveness. Clients who do not deal with their preparers' questions or return calls, questionnaires, or forms promptly set a negative tone and increase the accountant's time in looking for the information, following up, and incurring excessive "touches" of the client's files. Clients expect you to fully explain the fee arrangements before the work commences, advise them of additional services not anticipated (and associated fees for those services), and bill them promptly so it is clear what they owe. Clients then have the responsibility to pay the bill promptly. That is an easy and extremely effective way for the client to say, "Thank you for a job I appreciate." If a client needs the return for a specific purpose other than the obvious reason, he or she should inform the preparer and make clear the date and number of additional copies needed. Clients are expected to retain their tax information and the copies of returns provided to them. Clients who request extra copies of prior returns because they are too lazy to look for their copies make the accounting firm incur a cost, which should be passed on to the client. Many times, I have been asked for copies, and when I inform the clients of the charge, they tell me to skip it and that they will look in their files and make their own copies.

Clients have a right, as the customer, to be as demanding as they feel necessary, but their failure to reciprocate waters down the preparers' enthusiasm and, possibly, response time and increases the costs of the services for which they rely on us.

How to Determine Your Fees 19

Clients pay for a product—a tax return. They pay for a service—advice, counsel, and guidance. They also pay for an intangible—assurance of an exceptional job, the professional's attention to and focus on their matters, the assurance that the accountant will be around to deal with problems that might arise, and a secure feeling that they are getting the right help and doing the right things.

How do you charge for the things clients pay for? Do you bill each separately or bundle them into one number? Do you charge strictly by the amount of time it takes to prepare a return? Do you charge for the value you create when there are "outside the box" issues and efforts?

Some billing methods are as follows:

- Usually you charge what you can get.
- Same as last year (SALY).
- SALY with a slight increase.
- Fixed fee based on what the return should cost the client. (How much do you charge a client you've had for 15 years versus a new client for the exact same tax return?)
- Fee based on a chart, depending on the forms used and countable transactions.
- Time based on rates for level of staff.
- Time based, plus a computer or overhead charge, or both.
- Value bill based on what you did for the client. (Circular 230 doesn't permit this for tax preparation.)
- Success fee for extraordinary results you achieved. (Circular 230)
- Competitive amount based on what others charge.
- Part of the annual service to the client's business, with no extra billing or a nominal fee billed.
- How much do you charge for a client's college-age child who had four summer jobs in three different states?

- How do you value the intangible advice and feelings your clients get by using you?

How many times in your career did a client say that he or she wanted to buy such and such number of hours from you?

In many circumstances, tax returns from one year to the next are similar, without much change in the clients' situations. In those cases, a fee consistent with the previous year is appropriate, with small increases each year to offset some of the effects of inflation. In some cases, even those small increases do not occur. The reasons for this are many and are subject to many variables, such as the following:

1. A fee that creeps up annually and becomes higher than you would charge for new clients in the same situation. This creates a situation in which your loyal, long-term clients pay more than new clients with the same circumstances—not a healthy climate. Either the fee you are charging the new client is too low or you are overcharging your current clients. This has to be assessed, and something needs to be adjusted. Usually, the new client is getting a bargain or a low-ball fee that won't provide you with the appropriate income you need to earn. It would be better to charge the correct fee up front, rather than taking on the client at the lower starting fee. These decisions should be looked at from a macro viewpoint, and I have found that unless you will be adding a high volume at the lower fee, it is better to decline the lower paying clients while keeping your current fee structure and policy in place for your ongoing clients.
2. A fee does not match the increase in complexity of the return because of changing tax laws specifically related to that client's return. This problem is fixed by a one-time step up in the fee.
3. A fee that doesn't allow for extra work that has stealthily increased. Examples of this are when the client provides fewer summaries, causing a greater amount of work by you before you can get started on the tax return; increased stock transactions by the client; or the client making new investments in hedge funds that provide 30-plus page K-1s. A meeting with the client is in order to increase the fee; add the charges for the additional work; or have the client, when possible, do more of the preparatory work himself or herself.

4. A fee that doesn't indicate special work done in a particular year because no precedent was set, you feel loyalty to the client, or you don't want to have a confrontation. Either way, you are not getting paid for the services you are providing, which is similar to a butcher giving away free meat to a customer that is having a one-time dinner party. You need to monitor the work for your clients and bill for the extras or, minimally, advise the client before you start the work that there will be additional charges.
5. A fee that doesn't reflect the value added to a transaction or the super creative work done by you that leads to a significant benefit to the client. This doesn't necessarily have to be directly related to a transaction reported on the tax return. Instead, it could be initiating a meeting between a client who tells you that he or she is looking for a new job and a client looking for a partner to start a new business, in which the person looking for the job gets an ownership interest in the business by joining it. The value was provided to both clients. What will your bill be for: the two 15 minute phone calls you made or your 30 years of experience that enabled you to recognize the opportunity presented to both clients?

Be aware that tax preparation cannot have value or benefits created as a consideration for setting the fee after the return is completed. However, any method of value pricing can be used to set the fee before work on the return starts. Tax return fees cannot be based on results.

A word about fees: I may seem to be spending a lot of time talking about fees, but so should you. Hopefully, you will glean some ideas on how to increase your earnings, and some of those earnings will be for services that will provide significant value to your clients. Please refer to exhibit 19-1 in order to analyze your own practice.

EXHIBIT 19-1

What Business Are You In?

- ❑ Tax preparation.
- ❑ Accounting practice that does tax returns for individual clients.
- ❑ Financial services.
- ❑ I have a professional accounting practice and perform whatever services our clients indicate they need.
- ❑ I have an accounting business and will offer whatever services my clients indicate they need. I also try to let them know what they should be asking us to do for them and how we can help them better their financial situation and build long term financial security.
- ❑ Other: ______________________________

How Satisfied Are You With Your Practice or Business?

- ❑ My business is the right size for me.
- ❑ I would like my business to be larger so I could make more money.
- ❑ I would like to expand by building a much larger business.
- ❑ I think my practice is a little too big to handle the way I would like to handle it.
- ❑ Other: ______________________________

Are You Happy With Your Business's Growth Over the Last Five Years?

- ❑ Yes.
- ❑ No.

Are You Making More Money and Having More Fun Than You Did Five Years Ago?

- ❑ Yes.
- ❑ No.

Do you wish your answers were different?

What Do You Think Are the Most Critical Issues Affecting Your Practice?

1. ____
2. ____
3. ____
4. ____
5. ____

Two Letters to Send to Clients

Following are two letters demonstrating approaches that you can use to increase your tax fees. You don't have to use the letter if you will either see or talk to the client before tax season begins. It would be good business and a courteous effort to communicate with the client early enough so that he or she has time to engage a new preparer, if he or she so chooses.

Letter to Inform a Client of a Fee Increase for the Coming Year

Dear Client:

Over the years, we have valued your business and appreciated the opportunity to act as your tax advisor and return preparer.

Recent years, however, have brought with them ever increasing costs of providing these services to you. Costs such as maintaining a highly skilled and qualified staff, together with the technology needed to support them, as well as the effects of inflation, have made it impossible for us to maintain your fee at the current level.

As a result, we have been left with no choice but to increase your fee to $XXXX, starting with preparation of your 20XX income tax returns.

This has not been an easy decision for us, but as professional financial advisors, we must look at this decision in a purely business setting.

We hope that you will continue to see the value of our services and will understand the need for us to increase the fee associated with the high quality services we perform for you.

If you wish to discuss this matter with us, please do not hesitate to call.

Thank you in advance for your understanding.

Cordially,

Partner, CPA

Letter to Inform a Client of a Minimum Fee That Is Higher Than They Should Pay

Dear Client,

We have reviewed our fee structure for individual tax returns and have decided to impose a minimum charge of $XXX[1] per return for the 20XX tax season.

In reviewing your tax return and the fee we charged you, we feel that you can best be served by a colleague of ours who charges fees consistent with the way you have been billed in the past. Accordingly, we have made arrangements with a local CPA, Mr. Alfred Accountant, 123 Main Street, Your City, NJ Tel 1-XXX-XXX-XXXX, to provide him with our copies of your files and computer database, if you authorize us to do so.

We appreciate you using our services in the past and the trust you placed in us. We are confident that the quality of service and responsiveness that Mr. Accountant will provide will meet your high expectations.

We will provide Mr. Accountant with your contact information, but we will retain your files until we receive authorization from you to release the information. If you decide to use someone else, rest assured that we will cooperate with you in the transfer. Additionally, we will be available to discuss with you or your new accountant anything that appeared on the returns we prepared.

We thank you for your previous business and wish you a success in the future.

Cordially,

Partner, CPA

[1] Minimum not applicable to minor children's tax returns.

If you don't regularly increase your fees, please read the following story about Freddie the Barber.

A Cute but True Story

Freddie the Barber

I have been going to Freddie for haircuts for approximately 20 years. During that time, he has raised his price twice: from $10 to $12 and then to $15. The last increase was approximately 6 years ago. My tips were the same until approximately 3 years ago when I increased them from $3 to $5.

How does Freddie make more money?

It seems to me that he isn't making enough money to cover what have to be his increased costs. So, he has to be falling behind from what he was making 6 years ago and probably from what he was making 20 years ago.

We can suppose that he is getting more customers, but that doesn't cut it (no pun intended). First of all, he doesn't seem any busier now than he was six years ago, and he works in a salon, so he can't advertise his services. Second, he can't increase the amount of time he works. He works five days per week from 8 A.M. to 5 P.M. (off Sundays and Mondays). He can possibly work one night per week, but nine hours per day on your feet is tough. Third, maybe he can sell his customers additional services, such as hair coloring or a shave, or have his customers come in more often (my hair is not getting longer or thicker).

Maybe he can't do anything, so he just has to cut back on his spending.

Now, change Freddie's name to yours and change him from a barber to an accountant. Are your fees keeping up with your increased costs? Are you maxing out your pension and 401(k) plans? Have you cut back on nonessential expenses, such as vacations, or are things the same in that area? Are you working much harder now than you were in the past, and are you working harder than you want to work?

> Now is a good time to review your fees and consider increases. You may also want to weed out your two or three worse clients to make room for newer; more profitable; and, possibly, more pleasant and appreciative clients. Let us know about your experiences.

The Danger of Raising Fees

A definite danger exists in increasing fees: you can possibly lose the client. However, a definite danger also exists in not increasing fees: you will continue to make less as long as costs increase. You can get more business, but as we can see with Freddie's story that is usually not what happens, especially if you are bogged down in work without relief. So, let's see what actually results if you raise fees and lose business.

If you increase your fees by 40 percent, is it likely that you would lose more than 40 percent of your business? Probably, but let's get a little more serious. If you increase your fees by 10 percent, is it likely you would lose more than 10 percent of your business? Probably not. So, an increase of 10 percent can provide the same revenue if you lose the same percentage of business. However, with 10 percent less work to do, you just added inventory that could be used to increase billable services to existing clients, do a better job on existing clients, prospect for more business, or just take off some pressure. Also, with the reduced work, you would achieve some minor reductions in costs.

Minimum Fee Schedule

Following is a suggested minimum fee schedule that you can provide to prospective clients. It can also be used to price out the returns you do. When you construct the schedule, determine a fee for the basic return and then estimate the relationship of each schedule and form. After the fee schedule is done, test it by pricing out a few returns you did in the past and see how close it comes (or how far away). I developed this method after a few years of practicing when relatives, friends, and close associates asked me to do their tax returns and then had sticker shock when I told them the fee or when they got the bill after I did the work.

Once I had created the schedule, I simply told people that I would send them my fee schedule so they would have an idea of what the returns would cost, and I told them that they if they wished to use me, they could call my office for an appointment. If any reader would like a copy of the fee schedule in a Word file, e-mail me, and I'll reply with the attachment. This will save you from retyping and formatting it.

A B & C Associates, CPAs

MINIMUM FEE SCHEDULE

For individual income tax returns with gross incomes up to $125,000.

If all information needed to prepare return is not provided at initial meeting, there will be additional charges.

Client ______________ **Date** _________ **Tax Year** ______

Personal Return				***Other Schedules***		
Federal and State return with Schedule A	.00			Moving Expenses (3903)	.00	
Federal and State return with Standard Deduction	.00			Employee Bus. Exp. (2106)	.00	
Additional State Return	.00			Alimony Paid or Received	.00	
Part year/change of residency	.00			Exemption Release (8332)	.00	
Children's Short Return	.00			Casualty Loss (4684)	.00	
Kiddie Tax Calculation	.00			Education Expense (2106)	.00	
Parent's Election (8814)	.00			Estimated Tax (1040ES)	.00	
Excess (over 5) W-2's _____ @$ .00				Estimated tax calculation, done with return	.00	
				—done quarterly, minimum	.00	

(continued)

Schedules C & F				Underpayment Penalty (2210)	.00	
Business or Farm Income	.00			—annualization calculation	.00	
Self-Employment Tax Sch. SE	.00			Extension of Time to File, client supplies #	.00	
Depreciation Schedule	.00			Ext. where we calculate tax, minimum	.00	
—_____ @ $.00 per item				Tax on Tip Income (4137)	.00	
Home Office Deduction	.00			Net Operating Losses	.00	
				At Risk Limitation (6198)	.00	
Schedule D Transactions				Investment Interest (4952)	.00	
Stock Sales (first 5)	.00			Foreign Income (2555)	.00	
Excess _____ @ $.00 per item				Deceased T/P refund (1310)	.00	
Section 1244 Loss, per item	.00			Alternative Minimum Tax (6251)	.00	
Bad Debt Loss, per item minimum	.00					
Sale of collectibles	.00			***Tax Credits***		
Sale of Residence (2119)	.00			Low Income Housing Credit	.00	
Form 4797	.00			Credit for Elderly Sch. R	.00	
Installment Sale (6252) First Year	.00			Child Care Credit (2441)	.00	
subsequent Years (each)	.00			Recapture of Inv. Tax Cr. (4255)	.00	

Tax Deferred Exchange, minimum	.00			Foreign Tax Credit (1116)	.00	
Capital Loss Carryover	.00			Earned Income Credit	.00	
Repossess. & Foreclosures, minimum	.00			AMT credit	.00	
				Tax paid to other States	.00	
Other Income Items						
Schedule B (first 5)	.00			***Other Items***		
Excess _____ @ $.00 per item				Electronic Filing	no chg.	
Foreign Bank Acct. (TD F90-22.1)	.00			Amended Prior Year tax return, minimum	.00	
Rental Property (1st) (Sch. E)	.00			Compute W-4 Allowance	.00	
Add'l. Rentals (each)	.00			Extra Copy of Return, when return is prepared	.00	
Depreciation Schedule	.00			—after return is prepared	.00	
—plus _____ @ $.00 per item				Tax notice fixed fee pd. when return is prep.	.00	
Partnership, Trust (each K-1), minimum	.00			Tax notice responses, per hour	.00	
Unreimb. partnership expenses, minimum	.00			Postage and handling		no chg.

(continued)

Personal Return				***Other Schedules***		
Passive Loss Limit (8582)	.00			Express or messenger charges		
Passive Loss Allocations ____ @ $				Tel. call(s) to get additional info: ____ @	.00	
Taxability of Social Security	.00			Consulting ____ @ $ /hour		
Gambling income ____ @ $ per item				Consulting ____ @ $ /hour		
Gambling losses	.00			Accounting svces. for Sch. C or E	Per quote	
Pension Items						
Pension Income	.00					
Compute Non-Taxable Portion	.00					
IRA (non-deductible contri. Form 8606)	.00			Total charges	$	
Keogh or SEP calculation	.00			20% surcharge if Organizer not filled out*		
Rollover to IRA, per account	.00			*not applicable first year we do return		
Excise tax on Pension, IRA or				**TOTAL FEE**	$	
Keogh distribution (5329)	.00			***Minimum fee (except for a child's return)***	***$0.00***	

2/4/XX Name, address, telephone, fax, and email information goes here and on next line if needed.

Official IRS Instructions Booklets

Forms not included.

Tax preparation is complex, continuously changing, and performed under stressful conditions. The IRS's official instruction booklets are a testament to the difficulty of knowing the rules of engagement. Following are the covers of the most used instruction booklets, with the page count for 2013. Preparers are skilled professionals. They should have high self-esteem and be able to convey their skills and knowledge to their clients. Yet, many preparers sell themselves short with cut-rate fees.

The "long form" 1040 instruction book has 206 pages (without any forms). The "short form" 1040A instruction book is 88 pages. The 1040EZ, a baby brother or sister of the short form, is a 42-page instruction book. These page totals get higher every year.

...and the client expects to continue paying what you have been charging him or her for the last four years?

And you do!

Increasing Tax Return Fees

Try to increase the fees annually at least to cover your increased costs. I don't consider these as fee raises, but a method of passing on increased costs to the clients. Here is an illustration of the added cumulative revenue from regular increases, even modest increases.

	Raise 4%/yr	No increases
Year 1	$ 2,500	$ 2,500
Year 2	2,600	2,500
Year 3	2,730	2,500
Year 4	2,839	2,500
Year 5	2,952	2,500
Total collected	$13,541	$12,500
Increased revenues	$ 1,041	
Percent increase	8.3%	

If you haven't increased your fees, will you ever?

At what point?

Why not now?

With no fee increases and with increased costs, you will lose ground.

Accounting Fees

This is a reprint of a blog I posted on April 17, 2014, at www.partners-network.com regarding tax return fees, and is included to indicate the differences in the levels of service, fees relative to work done, and value delivered to the client.

...Actually, any type of professional fees. Accountants, lawyers, physicians, and even plumbers' fees—many clients complain they are too high.

Surprise! They are not too high. If they were, then many would retire much earlier than they do, take more vacations or have bigger houses and more expensive cars. Professionals usually earn good livings, but that is what they are—a living. Would you trust your work to a professional that did not earn a decent living? I think not!

The problem with fees is that they are for services, not for tangible products that many times can be compared to similar products widely sold in many places.

What is a service worth? I also know that it is difficult is compare two professional's fees for the same deliverable. Let's take a lawyer's one-hour consultation. One charges $200 and the other charges $600. Would the advice be the same making the service a commodity thereby making the attorney with the $200 fee the better value? Well, suppose the lawyer charging $200 has very little experience in the issues discussed while the lawyer charging $600 is a recognized national expert. Wouldn't you think the attorney with the higher fee would provide better guidance than the lawyer with the lower price? Suppose the consultation was for a life-altering strategy; wouldn't you want to meet with the most experienced attorney rather than the least expensive?

With respect to tax returns, two accountants can deliver the exact same return, while one charges $800 and the other $1,200. Might you think the accountant charging the $1,200 was priced too high? However, suppose I tell you that the lower-priced return was prepared after the information was mailed in with a brief call by the accountant, while the higher-priced return included a meeting with a CPA that resulted in suggestions to change the client's investment configuration to make it more tax efficient, some tips to give charity in a more efficient manner, advice to open a one-person 401(k) to shelter consulting income in the current year, and a heads up to sign up for their employer's cafeteria health plan for the next year. The return is the same. The advice is not! You evaluate the fee based on value received. Perhaps the fee for the $800 return should have been lower, while the advice provided should have been priced higher. Either way, professional services and fees are not necessarily subject to comparison.

I suggest that every bill you receive be considered a value bill. Consider the value received and either shop around for a new professional or be glad you had access to a great professional at a bargain price.

Expectation Gap 20

The Difference Between What You and Your Clients Expect

No matter how you organize your processes, many unexpected things crop up. The frequency and timing of the unexpected events almost make many of them expected. Because of the nature of dealing with the public and their concentrated concerns about the work being done for them, and you having a practice and juggling the interests of your many clients, gaps can develop between what you and the client expect. Following is a depiction of the gaps in expectations:

What Clients Expect

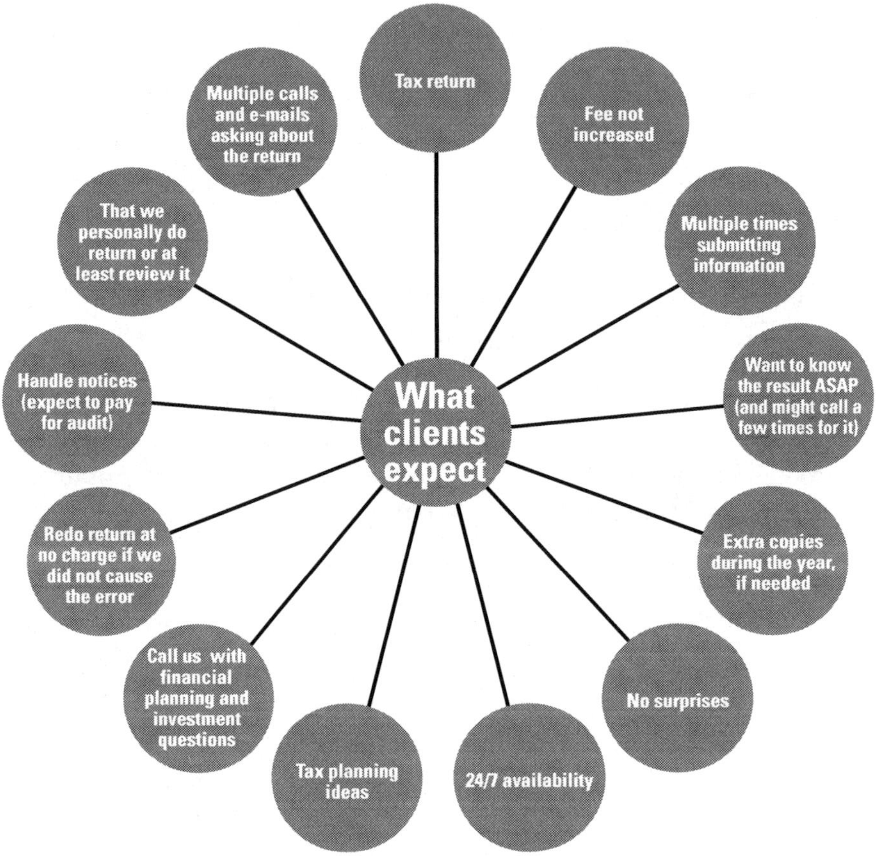

What We Expect

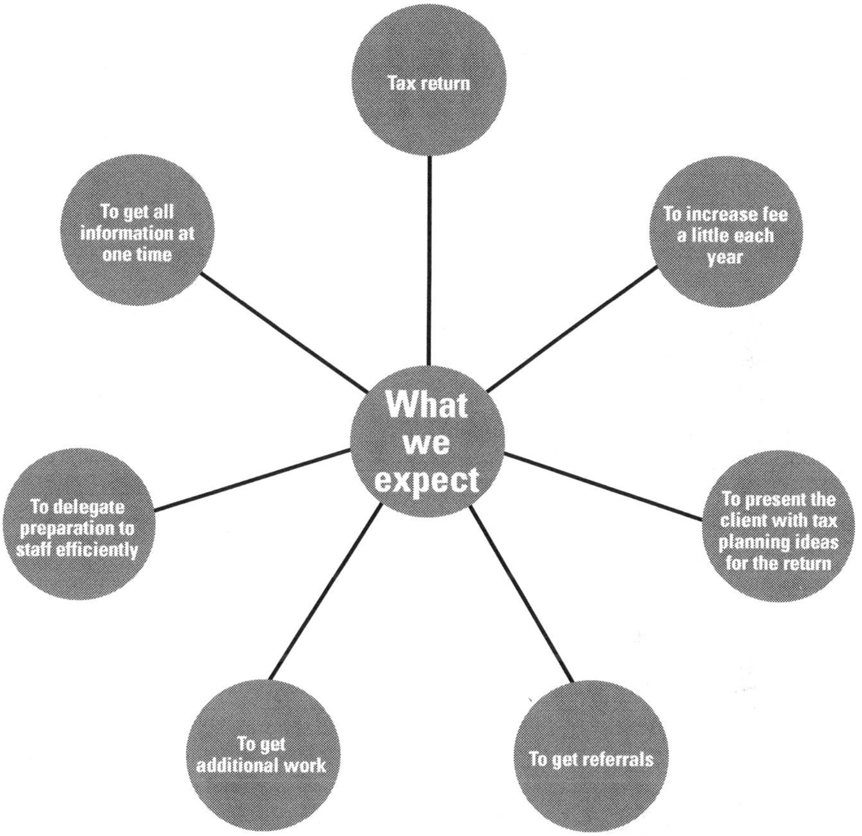

Unless you run a tax preparation mill in which the clients come in or drop off their information and get a completed tax return with little or no contact with you or a professional from your office, clients expect certain things that they assume are part of the process. Clients may question initial fees, but not the process of increasing them or billing for extras. Clients don't consider the effects on your office or the added time when they do not provide all the information at the initial interview or time of submission but send it in piecemeal. On the other hand, accountants always assume, unrealistically, that they will get all the information at one time. Although you know you will delegate the work to the appropriate level staff person, the client assumes the partner will do the entire return himself or herself. To address this gap in expectations, you should explain your office's preparation and staff delegation process while assuring the client that nothing will leave the office without your supervision and review and that he or she can always call you directly with any questions. This explanation is also important if a staff person needs to call a client to get additional information or clear up an issue.

Many accountants expect referrals from clients but never ask for them. To the contrary, many accountants give the impression that they are overworked, harried, can't comfortably handle the work they have, or are shorthanded. These are all images that thwart referrals, even if the client wanted to and had the opportunity to refer you. The same goes for getting additional work from your clients. Tax clients won't turn to you for additional services unless they think you have the time to do them and know that you perform such services. See chapter 21 on introducing tax clients to additional services for suggestions about the types of extra services with which you can assist clients. Also, as professional accountants, you should offer an elevated service and distinguish yourself from tax preparation firms. The main way to do so is to present tax planning ideas to your clients. Without this elevated service, you offer no added value to the client. Rather, you are a supplier of a commodity that is best handled by the lowest cost provider, which, overall, provides the best value because commodities are sold by price. Clients expect elevated services, too, so what have you done, or what are you doing, about this? One thing you can do is list the planning ideas you have presented to clients during tax season then review them to determine to which additional clients you can suggest these ideas. Look at what I wrote about 1/20 rule in chapter 21 to better serve clients.

Clients never like surprises and don't expect them. A way to avoid surprises is to prepare projections before the year ends. Further, if a result on the final return is quite different than what you believe a client is expecting, based on the projection or from separate discussions with the client, call the client as soon as you are sure of the amount and explain the reason. Also, leave yourself a little wiggle room by telling the client that you will send him or her a summary (see the worksheets I described in chapter 12) and go over it after he or she has had a chance to review it. This will give the client time for the result to sink it and become familiar. Clients expect and deserve their calls and e-mails to be responded to timely, but they don't expect 24/7 availability, unless you are in the habit of responding to e-mails in the middle of the night and on weekends. Then, you become their 24/7 accountant. Is that what you want? Clients expect to call us whenever they have a financial planning and investment question. That is okay and should be encouraged, but you need to be paid for your time responding to their questions. If you don't bill on time, and don't want to send a bill each time, then consider adding an extra amount on the tax return bill for financial planning services performed during the year. It works. I know this for sure.

An easy way to bill for added services and calls during the year is to add an amount on the tax return bill with wording similar to the following.

Financial planning services during the year $XXX.XX

The fee could be approximated based on your hourly rate. For instance if a client called you five times during the year with investment, financial, or tax questions and you estimate that each call lasted about 10 minutes, then bill for an hour or almost an hour and if the client questions it, tell him or her it covered your time for the five or so times he or she called you. The separate itemization will distinguish this from the tax preparation fee. See prior chapter on billing.

Introducing Tax Clients to Additional Services 21

Using Your Tax Work to Expand Your Practice

Part of growing a practice is to have existing clients use more of your services. A major goal of every meeting with a client is to make sure that the client knows every way you can help him or her with his or her relevant issues. These opportunities can come from anyone in the firm. Therefore, it is important for each person in the firm to understand what the firm can do and how it can offer relevant services to the client. Accomplishing this goal requires careful, directed, and focused training.

What would you think of a dentist that did not tell you that you needed special gum work only to find out on your own when a bunch of your teeth needed to be pulled because of gum disease? Or a physician that did not explain why it was necessary for you to reduce your sugar intake because you were on the verge of diabetes? Well, what would clients think of you if you did not warn them that their overall investments were not going to enable them to reach the retirement goals they told you about? I believe we, as professionals and trusted advisors, have the responsibility to inform clients of the need for additional services from us that would enable them to attain their goals, increase their financial security or invest in a more tax-efficient manner. That's what this chapter is about. It is not about us making more money, although that is what would occur, but it is about us helping clients realize their dreams.

The largest volume of clients is usually for tax return services. The tax return interview to gather information is a tremendous opportunity to find out the client's concerns and how you can help him or her. It is also an opportunity to provide a life changing benefit to the client while increasing your revenues.

The tax return interview opportunities are as follows:

- One hour opening envelopes versus "free" personalized financial guidance. I refer to sitting with a client while the client organizes his or her data, which should have done before the meeting, as *opening envelopes*.
- Be interested in the client, ask about his or her concerns, and really listen.
- Get the client to articulate what he or she cares about and what keeps him or her awake at night.
- The client comes completely organized, with a list of financial planning and business questions that he or she would like you to answer.

Upgrade Your Tax Clients

Some of your tax preparation clients could be upgraded to pre-year-end planning and projections. Others can have planning and review meetings in the summer. The extra meeting also leaves some time to chat in an unrushed atmosphere that tax season cannot provide. That discussion could also lead to additional services. Firms that offer financial services, such as annuities, mutual funds, insurance, mortgages, and even immediately opened IRA accounts, can give a very brief mention if they feel the client would benefit from these products. Some offer outsourced bookkeeping and CFO services that can be easily pointed out. Some preparers try to get involved advising with their clients' stock options and compensation packages. Whatever your skill level and clients' needs, opportunities exist.

I give an annual financial planning speech and print extra handouts to present to tax clients if the subject comes up at the tax information gathering meeting. This raises their awareness of my (and my firm's) expertise and also gives them a usable guide that covers many of their concerns. Even if you don't write or present a speech, many inexpensive financial planning booklets can prominently feature your firm's name. Booklets are also available on a myriad of other topics. I find that these are instant image upgrades.

Types of Additional Services

The following checklist of services can give you ideas of what clients might need as well as serve as a guide to the type of services you can perform.

1. Estate planning
2. Inheritance advice and guidance
3. Succession planning
4. Personal financial planning
5. Investment allocation construction
6. Investment management
7. Investment clubs
8. Elder care assurance services
9. Business performance measurement services
10. QuickBooks training and consulting
11. Outsourced business and back office services
12. Outsourced CFO services
13. Outsourced corporate tax preparation, such as income taxes, executive tax preparation, sales taxes, and state registrations
14. Second opinions
15. Business valuations
16. Retirement planning and counseling
17. Pension planning
18. IRA distribution analysis
19. IRS tax audit protection service
20. Conflict resolution
21. Planning for single couples living together
22. Second marriage assistance
23. Prenuptial agreement analysis
24. Divorce settlement planning
25. Conflict resolution
26. Buying and selling a business
27. Starting a business
28. Buying a franchise
29. Entering a partnership
30. Getting stock in a corporation
31. Receiving stock options
32. Projecting financial aspects of proposed actions

33. Basis calculations for pass-through activities
34. Employment contract negotiations
35. Executive compensation review
36. Downsize settlement structuring
37. Corporate management and financial planning training
38. Industry specific tax and business advisory services
39. Structuring partnership and buy sell agreements
40. Recession consulting

This list is not complete, but it is a good start for you to start thinking about what types of additional services you can offer to your clients.

Ways to Make Clients Aware of Your Capabilities

The following is a short list of the many areas in which you can help clients. Go over the preceding list of 40 areas and apply as many as you can to each client and then target the top 1/20 to call and offer your help.

1. Call your clients after tax season and ask them to come in for a consultation:
   a. A suggestion is to call a client in June and tell the client that you are reviewing his or her financial situation and that you feel he or she could be helped by a high value low cost consultation to review his or her asset allocation and goals to make sure they match up (a fiscal fitness checkup). Mention a fixed amount for a 90 minute consultative meeting.
   b. *1/20 rule.* A suggestion is to target meetings with 1/20 of your eligible tax preparation clients each year. This is an opportunity to help them and to elevate your service beyond the preparation of their tax returns. Note that you will have to call much more than 1/20 of your clients to get meetings with 5 percent of them, but it will be well worth the effort.

Use the Ed Mendlowitz 1/20 rule to better serve clients.

   c. An eligible client excludes school age children or clients in nursing homes and, possibly, someone just filing bankruptcy. Actually, the bankrupt client might really need your help in rehabilitating his or her credit standing and adjusting his or her spending habits. If he or she is a long term client, you could do this on a pro bono basis because there's nothing wrong with helping someone every once in a while.
2. When your clients come in to provide you with their tax information, tell them what services are available as you review their information:
   a. An example is if they need retirement planning or help with their 401(k) investment allocation choices.
   b. Another hot area is IRA conversions to Roth IRAs.
   c. An important service is assembling all the client's investment statements and doing a cohesive and comprehensive asset allocation analysis. Most clients have the analysis done piecemeal by brokerage account or custodian, and you need to tell them about this option.
3. Engage your clients and be interested in them. Find out their long term goals, not just financial goals. Find out who they know that you know or would like to meet:
   a. Calling your clients to pass on information creates a bond that you might be able to use later on to help them or yourself.
4. Relate what you do for your client's job and industry or company:
   a. If the client works for a small manufacturer, distributor, or advertising agency, let him or her know that you have a lot of clients who are small manufacturers, distributors, or advertising agencies and tell him or her about your consulting services in those areas, including cost control, inventory control, or exploiting expansion or bank finance opportunities.
   b. If the client works for a closely held family business, tell him or her about (i) your expertise in advising families in succession planning or training younger family members in basic business techniques; (ii) how you can help the owner develop exit strategies, including preparing the business for sale; or (iii) how you can perform due diligence if the owner is thinking of expanding by buying a competitor or entering a new market.

  c. If the client is a business executive, tell him or her how you can help with employment contracts or obtaining high- or executive-level perks, such as stock options or restricted stock.

5. Other areas in which you can offer to assist clients are as follows:
   a. Discuss their interest and dividend 1099s to determine why they chose those investments, and based on their responses, make them aware of possible alternatives, including tax exempt bonds, annuities, or preferred stocks. (Note that I am not recommending any of these by this mention.)
   b. You can discuss goals, such as how concerned the client is about educational funding for his or her children or grandchildren, as well as the client's own retirement and financial security when he or she no longer works.
   c. If the client is supporting a relative, has the client made adequate arrangements should the client die prematurely? Does the client have the right documents, such as a will, trusts, and guardianship payment or "allowance" arrangements?
   d. When was the last time the client reviewed his or her IRA and 401(k), 403(b), pension, and similar plan beneficiary designations, if ever? In some cases, doing so could be more important than having a will. You could be the right person for the client to speak to or the catalyst to have these items put in order, so the client can accomplish what he or she really wants.
   e. Clients who are charity minded can be assisted to make sure that adequate funds are left to their favorite organizations in the right manner.
   f. Clients with over- or under withholding can be assisted to adjust these amounts. Also, at that time, the underlying circumstances causing those situations can be reviewed and, perhaps, beneficially altered.
   g. Clients with household employees and nannies can be walked through the proper requirements for reporting the wages paid.
   h. When a marital separation or divorce is contemplated.

Cross-Selling

Courtesy of WithumSmith+Brown

Busy season. It's a 120-day fire drill chock-full of deadlines, demands, and a to-do list that is as long as the office dinner orders. On the positive side, it's also your chance to take advantage of outstanding opportunities to cross-sell new services to your number one target—your client.

Successful marketing is always about targeting the right audience, at the right time, with the right message. As their trusted advisor, your meetings with clients present the ripest moment to discuss the most top-of-mind topics, such as the challenges your clients are currently facing, new initiatives planned for the upcoming year, and other business and financial concerns they may have.

With some advanced planning, you can net some new engagements. Even if you don't, rest assured that you can use the discussion to strengthen your relationship by showing your clients that you care about them.

1	**Do a little homework.** All clients consider themselves to be part of a business niche. What current dynamics are facing their industry? What challenges are imposed? What are their competitors doing? Consider the range of accounting and consulting services you offer and how that may fit into your clients' potential needs, based on this research. Your preparation will enable a well-informed discussion and help them identify gaps in their own infrastructure.
2	**Enlist the right internal experts.** If you've identified a gap or need your client (or their industry) is facing, be sure to talk to those who specialize in the key areas in advance of the meeting. They can help you structure the conversation and provide you with the information you need. Don't feel pressured to be an expert on every facet of accounting. Enlisting the right resources will greatly benefit you, and your client will appreciate knowing there is specialized knowledge within the firm.
3	**Schedule additional time.** As you schedule the year-end meeting to review the tax or audit engagement, plan for an additional 20–30 minutes for the cross-sell discussion. It will allow you enough time for your client to open up, and it will provide you with just enough time for a light pitch. Remember, you don't need to close the deal in this meeting; you just need to create a warm lead for new service opportunities. You can plan the follow-up process once the seed has been planted.
4	**Do a short run-through.** Find a colleague known for his or her candor and ask him or her to play the role of client. Then, take him or her through your pitch. In as little as 15 minutes, you can increase your confidence as he or she fires away with potential client questions or gives constructive feedback on your approach.

5	**Listen more than you speak.** When it comes to selling services, sometimes it is just better to listen. Your clients don't want to feel inundated with information or feel they are being manipulated at this meeting to take on more fees. As they vocalize their needs or concerns, they will begin the process of selling into themselves. Your job is to hear them out and then make suggestions on how the firm may help improve their pain points.
6	**Ask for client referrals or testimonials.** Happy clients are some of the best and most reliable resources for referrals. A good, solid testimonial will help you with a future sell-in. Although it may feel bold or uncomfortable at first, now is the time you can capture the testimonials because the clients are happiest with the service you provide.
7	**Bring along a less-experienced team member.** Sounds counterintuitive, right? Wrong. The best way to teach the art of selling services is through demonstration. The year-end closeout is a great opportunity for intimate client interaction. By involving junior talent, you will be developing your own legion of future marketers. In turn, they will not only appreciate the break from the mounds of paper on their desk but the chance to learn from you.
8	**Don't forget your internal sales.** Getting noticed internally for the right reasons is critical. For the junior staff, make sure the right people know the extra effort and dedication you are putting in to the year-end meeting. You don't need to brag, but you can display your interest and dedication as you identify potential client needs or cross-sell ideas. For partners, you can demonstrate through the sell-in process what it means to be a well-balanced CPA and growth driver for the firm. You are the example you set for junior staff on marketing, client relationships, and protocol.
9	**Use mealtimes as a meal ticket. Everyone needs to eat—even in busy season.** So, if you can't get the extra time tagged on to the year-end meeting, schedule a lunch or coffee break with clients for some discussion. Keep it friendly and informal, but let them know you are thinking about some of the challenges uncovered in the year-end process. You can even use these busy season mealtimes to meet with lawyers or bankers to keep your referral pipeline active. Nothing more energizing or nutritious than the prospect of some new business.
10	**Ask the marketing team for help.** Don't have time to do the research on a client or his or her industry? Want a little help finding the right angle? The marketing team is on hand to help do the homework you need to prepare for the meeting. In addition, they can lend a critical perspective on your pitch.

AICPA Standards in Personal Financial Planning Services

The AICPA *Statement on Standards in Personal Financial Planning Services No. 1* as adopted by the Personal Financial Planning Executive Committee became effective July 1, 2014, and applies to AICPA members who engage in the following service areas:

- Cash flow planning
- Risk management and insurance planning

- Retirement planning
- Investment planning
- Estate, gift, and wealth transfer planning
- Elder planning
- Charitable planning
- Education planning
- Tax planning

Many of these services are performed by tax preparers, especially the more experienced and those especially concerned with providing clients with added services. Further, many of the added services CPAs perform that are mentioned below fall under these categories.

It is recommended that the reader obtain a copy of the new standards, review it to determine whether they fall under its provisions and make every effort to comply with this statement.

Following is an illustration that indicates the broad scope of the statement.[1]

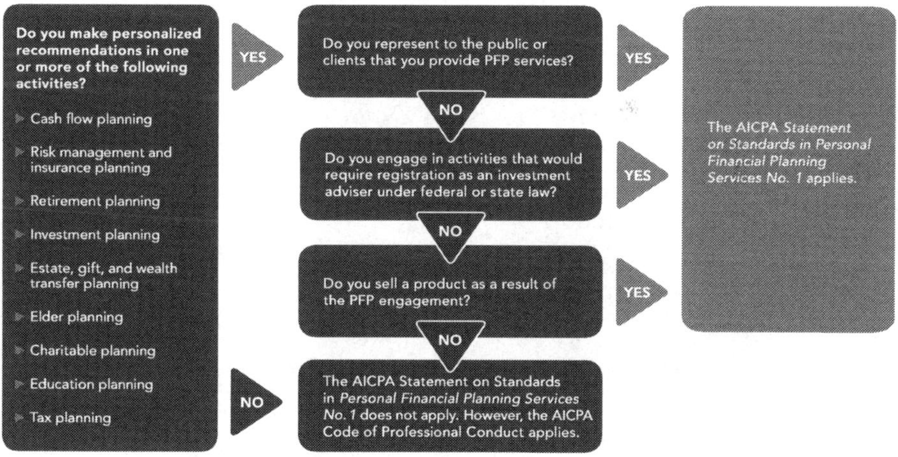

Following is a sample engagement letter included in the statement that you should consider using when offering such services.

[1] Source: AICPA PFP Section *Standards in Personal Financial Planning Services Compliance Toolkit*

Statement on Standards in Personal Financial Planning Services Sample Engagement Letter – General

This sample engagement letter provides nonauthoritative guidance to assist with compliance with Statement on Standards in Personal Financial Planning Services (SSPFPS) No. 1 (the statement) published by the American Institute of CPAs (AICPA). This engagement letter is intended to be customized to meet the needs of the member's practice and individual engagements (see "Notice to Readers" at the end of the letter). The member should review language used in the engagement letter in conjunction with reviewing requirements of the statement. This sample engagement letter should not be used for investment advisory relationships due to the legal and regulatory requirements of engagements involving investment advice.

[Date]

[Name and Address of Client]

Dear [Name of client]:

Introduction

We are looking forward to working with you in designing your personal financial plan. The personal financial planning process is complex. It is an important step toward achieving personal financial goals. This letter is to confirm our mutual understanding of the terms and objectives of our engagement to provide you with personal financial planning services as well as the nature and limitations of the services we will provide.

We will prepare your personal financial plan after consideration of your financial objectives and goals, and your present and forecasted financial situation. Our services will encompass the following activities [select appropriate options]:

- Cash flow planning
- Risk management and insurance planning
- Retirement planning
- Investment planning
- Estate, gift, and wealth transfer planning
- Elder planning
- Charitable planning
- Education planning
- Tax planning
- Other (specify)

The personal financial planning process requires your cooperation in providing us with various types of information and documents concerning your personal financial situation. We will be relying on your representations. If we are unable to obtain from you sufficient information to form a reasonable basis for conclusions and recommendations, our services in connection with this engagement may be limited to those matters for which sufficient information is available, and this may affect our conclusions and recommendations. Should this be the case, we will so advise you in writing.

If we are unable to obtain sufficient information to proceed with the engagement as contemplated and agreed, we will advise you and, as appropriate, discuss terminating or modifying the engagement with you. If we agree to modify or terminate the engagement, we will communicate that to you in writing.

We will keep your personal, non-public information strictly confidential. If your personal information needs to be disclosed when working with your other advisers or with other qualified professionals, we will ask your permission to do so. However, we may be required by legal or regulatory authorities to disclose confidential information without your permission.

Description of the Engagement

OPTION #1 (GENERAL)

Our approach to the personal financial planning process will proceed as follows:

- The initial phase involves accumulating and organizing facts about your current and desired financial status and identifying your specific goals and objectives. This will be accomplished through a series of interviews and the data-gathering questionnaire and use of our knowledge of you from prior services.
- The next step involves analysis of the data accumulated and a review with you of your cash flows.
- Following this review and further analysis, we will then make our preliminary recommendations. A written draft of your plan will be prepared and presented to you.
- We then will finalize your plan and set time goals and establish responsibilities for the implementation of the plan. We will prepare, in writing, specific recommendations that will seek to address your financial goals. When appropriate, we will include financial illustrations and projections for greater understanding of potential outcomes of financial alternatives.

We are available to assist you in implementing the actions and strategies agreed upon as you deem appropriate. The nature and extent of our implementation services will be established at that time. Implementation of your plan is a separate engagement, and we will provide you with a separate engagement letter for that process when and if that becomes necessary.

OPTION #2 (SPECIFIC)

Our approach to the personal financial planning process will include the following steps:

- We will schedule a preliminary meeting to assist you in defining short-term and long-term goals and to gather information about your family situation and major anticipated financial obligations.

- In addition to the quantitative data requested in our financial planning questionnaire, we will require copies of all pertinent documents, such as wills, trusts, investment holdings (and their cost bases), personal employment benefit statements, Social Security benefit statements, prior tax returns, and insurance coverages.
- We may require access to and discussions with your accountants, lawyers, insurance advisors, and other advisors or salespeople.
- After the information has been received, we will organize and review the data. We will analyze the quantitative information relating to tax liability (both income and estate), cash flow, net worth, risk management, and retirement. This should enable us to make appropriate projections with respect to your financial plan.
- Subsequent meetings may be required to verify the accuracy of the data and to allow you to validate the assumptions used in the projections. Our analysis and recommendations are based on information you provide, and it is essential that we receive correct information.
- Based on our analysis of the data, we will outline alternative strategies or courses of action to meet your immediate and long-term goals and objectives and to mitigate problems uncovered.
- At the conclusion of the engagement, we will prepare and discuss with you a report that includes our recommendations and projections.

We are available to assist you in implementing the actions and strategies agreed upon. The nature and extent of our implementation services will be established at that time. Implementation of your plan is a separate engagement, and we will provide you with a separate engagement letter for that process when and if that becomes appropriate.

Responsibility

In order to ensure that your personal financial plan contains sound and appropriate financial planning recommendations, it is your responsibility to provide complete and accurate information regarding all aspects of your personal and financial situation. Responsibility for financial planning decisions is yours. We will aid you in the decision-making process, suggest alternative recommendations to help you achieve your objectives, and assist you in determining how well each alternative meets your financial planning objectives.

The suggestions and recommendations included in your personal financial plan will be advisory in nature, and we cannot guarantee the performance of any investment or insurance products that may be purchased to implement recommendations in your plan. The plan will also include financial projections based on assumptions about future events. We cannot vouch for the achievability of such projections because the assumptions about future events may not prove to be accurate.

If in the course of this engagement we become aware of a service needed to complete the engagement that we do not or will not provide, we will advise you of that needed service and recommend to you in writing that you engage another service provider to address that service. If you decline to engage such recommended service provider, and we determine that such action impairs our ability to properly address the terms of this engagement, we will so advise you, in writing, and terminate this engagement. If you decline to engage such recommended service provider and we determine that our ability to properly address the terms of this engagement is not impaired, but may be limited in some way, we will advise you, in writing, with respect to how we believe our conclusions and recommendations may be affected.

We cannot be responsible for the acts, omissions, or solvency of any broker, agent, or independent contractor or other advisor or professional selected to implement any part of your personal financial plan. Our services are not designed, and should not be relied upon, as a substitute for your own business judgment nor are they meant to mitigate the necessity of your personal review and analysis of a particular investment. Our services are designed to supplement your own planning analysis and to aid you in fulfilling your financial objectives.

In addition, these services are not designed to discover fraud, irregularities, or misrepresentations made in materials provided to us concerning your potential investments or insurance coverages.

Other Service Providers

OPTION #1

In the event we refer you to another service provider, we will not receive any compensation, directly or indirectly, for making such a referral.

OPTION# 2

In the event we refer you to another service provider, we will disclose to you, in writing, any compensation we receive for making such a referral. We will [not] evaluate the work performed by the referred service provider.

OPTION #3

In the event we refer you to another service provider, we will disclose to you, in writing, any compensation we receive for making such a referral. We will, as part of our engagement, evaluate the work performed and the advice given by such service provider(s). If we do not concur with the advice provided by such service provider(s), we will communicate our nonconcurrence to you in writing.

Description of Fees

OPTION #1

Our estimated fee for the services previously described will be $[insert amount] plus out-of-pocket expenses. We will submit our bill monthly as services are performed, and it will be due and payable upon receipt. If an extension of our services is requested, we will discuss our fee arrangements at that time. Plan implementation as well as plan monitoring and updating, if needed, are separate engagements. If you choose one of these additional services, a separate engagement letter will be provided. These services will be billed separately.

OPTION #2

The fee for this planning service will be based on our regular hourly rates of $[insert amount] per hour, plus out-of-pocket expenses. We project our fee will range between $[insert amount] and $[insert amount], plus direct out-of-pocket expenses for the initial plan development. Plan implementation as well as plan monitoring and updating, if needed, are separate engagements. If you choose one of these additional services, a separate engagement letter will be provided. These services will be billed separately.

OPTION #3

Our estimated fee for the service previously described will be based on our standard hourly rates of $[insert amount] per hour and should range from $[insert amount] to $[insert amount]. We will submit our bill monthly, as services are performed, and it will be due and payable upon receipt. If an extension of our services is requested, we will discuss our fee arrangements at that time. Plan implementation as well as plan monitoring and updating, if needed, are treated as separate engagements. If you choose one of these additional services, a separate engagement letter will be provided. These services will be billed separately.

OPTION #4

The professional relationship described in this letter will be for 12 months, commencing on the date of this letter, and ending 12 months thereafter. Our compensation is based on a flat fee of $[insert amount]. Payment is due in three installments: $[insert amount] due with the acceptance of these terms, $[insert amount] due on [insert date], and $[insert amount] due on [insert date]. If an extension of our services is requested, we will discuss our fee arrangements at that time. Plan implementation as well as plan monitoring and updating, if needed, are as separate engagements. If you choose one of these additional services, a separate engagement letter will be provided. These services will be billed separately.

Conflicts of Interest [Refer also to "Other Service Providers"]

OPTION #1

We have no conflicts of interest in the acceptance of this engagement. We will advise you of any conflicts of interest, should they arise.

OPTION #2

We have a conflict of interest. [Insert description of conflict.] We will advise you of any other conflicts of interest, should they arise.

Concluding Remarks

You will, of course, be free to follow or disregard, in whole or in part, any recommendations we make. You are under no obligation to act on any recommendation. Because you did not engage us to assist you with the implementation of your personal financial plan, we cannot be responsible for any decisions you make regarding implementation of the recommendations. [Optional: At your request, we will be happy to coordinate implementation, as a separate engagement, with any insurance broker, investment broker, attorney, or other professional of your choosing.]

We will be pleased to discuss this letter with you at any time. If the foregoing is in accordance with your understanding, please sign one copy of this letter in the space provided and return it to us. The additional copy is for your files.

This engagement may be terminated without penalty or further obligation except for the payment of fees for services performed and expenses incurred prior to termination.

We agree that we will not assign this engagement without your prior written approval.

If we can be of assistance to you in any other way, please do not hesitate to contact us. We look forward to helping you develop and maintain a sound, businesslike approach to your personal financial affairs.

We thank you for the opportunity to be of service. We anticipate beginning the engagement sometime after [insert date]. If you have any questions, please call us at [insert phone number].

Very truly yours,

____

[Firm Name]

We agree to the terms of the engagement described in this letter.

____

[Client Name]

____

[Signature]

____

[Date]

Costs of Preparing a Tax Return 22

Worksheet to Calculate Your Costs

Shown in the following table are the items that go into the preparation of a typical individual tax return. You might not have the same items, or you might have some extra items. The point is that you should know all your costs, and the following is a good start. Note that some items need to be allocated, and some items are general overhead that would be allocated on a cost per return basis but are sunk costs and, perhaps, should not be marginally applied.

An example of the sunk costs is tax preparation software. Whether you do 1 return or 300, the cost is the same. There might be extra charges for certain state downloads, or a per-user fee, but for our discussion, let's assume the cost is $2,000 and you plan on doing 200 returns. That works out to a $10 cost per return. If your costing doesn't take that $10 into account, you are not getting a complete grasp on the cost of each return, and you might be pricing your returns too low. On the other hand, if you reach your expected 200 returns and are asked to "bid" to do a company's employees tax returns, you might not want to add that $10 as the cost because it involves no marginal costs to you, having already recovered your costs with the expected returns you prepared. So, understanding the costs is crucial to pricing your product. In the whole scheme of things, this may not be your most significant cost, but for a smaller practice, it is important.

(I have a sole practitioner friend who has a big tax practice and was using top-of-the-line preparation software. He decided to switch to a low-end product and used the savings to join a country club near his office so he could golf almost every day. The inconvenience he feels by not having better software is offset by his decreased handicap.)

No one ever hits their projected number of returns on the head. If you are under, then you have a slightly additional cost per return. If you do more returns, you make a little more on your overhead. Neither is a practice breaker. Some firms that bill on a cost plus basis, or that want to apportion their costs a little better, add a charge based on the size of the return or add a per-page charge to their time run for their clients.

Item	**Total Cost**	**Individual Return Cost** *(Divide aggregate cost by the number of tax returns you expect to do)*	**Unbillable Costs**
Tax software			
Special or dedicated hardware			
Paper and supplies			
Postage and express delivery services			
Messenger delivery			
Time preparing the return			
Review time			
Correcting return time for excessive errors			
Administrative staff time			
Remote access costs			
E-filing costs			
Tax return and software training			
Overtime pay, bonuses, or extra amounts included in staff salary			
Presents and "extras" to staff after tax season			
Client organizers			
Newsletters sent to tax clients			
Food for staff			
Bowling party, masseuse, ice cream party, and so on			
Handling, scanning, and returning client information			
Overhead allocation			

Greatest Cost Items

Now that you've done the exercise in the previous chart, let's take a look at your greatest cost item—personnel or time cost.

You need to aggregate the actual cost to you of your personnel or hourly cost. Add the annual salary, plus taxes, plus benefits, plus professional memberships and subscriptions, plus continuing education and training, plus reimbursements, plus possible overtime costs or tax season bonuses. Divide that total by the actual chargeable hours worked. If you have a 40-hour week and your staff works 45 weeks per year, you have an available inventory of 1800 hours per professional. You can add 400 overtime tax season hours to get 2200 available chargeable hours. Now, reduce that by the nonchargeable time—say 250 hours, leaving 1950 chargeable hours. If your total cost for a particular staff person is $85,000, your cost per hour is approximately $44. Your pay rate to that employee might be $30 per hour ($1200 per week for a 40-hour work week). If you've never done this, it could be a real eye opener. This calculation may reveal that paying overtime, even at time and a half, can be less expensive than adding a new person.

Item	Total Cost	Individual Return Cost	Unbillable Costs
Tax software			
Special or dedicated hardware			
Paper and supplies			
Postage and express delivery services			
Messenger delivery			
Time preparing the return			
Review time			
Correcting return time for excessive errors			
Administrative staff time			
Remote access costs			

(continued)

Item	Total Cost	Individual Return Cost	Unbillable Costs
E-filing costs			
Tax return and software training			
Overtime pay, bonuses or extra amounts included in staff salary			
Presents and "extras" to staff after tax season			
Client organizers			
Newsletters sent to tax clients			
Food for staff			
Bowling party, masseuse, ice cream party, and so on			
Handling, scanning, and returning client information			
Overhead allocation			

Recognize that personnel costs are your greatest cost items. What are you doing to reduce these costs?

One solution is better training and fewer touches and re-dos.

Marketing or Practice Development Costs

Some of the items on the tax return cost chart can be considered as marketing, making your firm more user-friendly and more pleasant to deal with. These costs help create a bond that firmly establishes the likelihood of that client returning every year for many, many years.

Item	Total Cost	Individual Return Cost	Unbillable Costs
Tax software			
Special or dedicated hardware			
Paper and supplies			
Postage and express delivery services			
Messenger delivery			
Time preparing the return			
Review time			
Correcting return time for excessive errors			
Administrative staff time			
Remote access costs			
E-filing costs			
Tax return and software training			
Overtime pay, bonuses, or extra amounts included in staff salary			
Presents and "extras" to staff after tax season			
Client organizers			
Newsletters sent to tax clients			
Food for staff			
Bowling party, masseuse, ice cream party, and so on			
Handling, scanning, and returning client information			
Overhead allocation			

What about calls to clients when you receive their information, ask for additional information, tell them what they will owe, or to discuss an unanticipated result?

Unbillable costs can include training; redoing returns because of excessive preparer errors; or improper scheduling, such as having a partner perform services that a much lower-level staff person could have done if he or she had been available.

One word about the costs: some systems capture and assign computer costs each time a return is run. If there are three re-dos (because of poor quality), the computer costs will be entered three times, distorting the actual costs. The same is true with other costs that are repetitive when there are re-dos. However, if a re-do is the client's fault, those captured costs will be correct, and you should consider an extra bill for that work. One such repetitive redo is because of corrected 1099s from brokerage accounts. Not our fault. Not the clients' fault. Who should pay for it? And why it is us? It is us when we do the additional work and don't charge for it.

It is good to know your costs and price them out to know how much to quote a job, but sometimes, it is not good business. An example happened to me a number of years ago when we were asked if we could do a job in which the fee would have averaged approximately 40 percent of our normal rates, and the value of the job was significantly greater. However, the job would have been done on our premises and could be done at odd hours and used as fill-in work. There would have been no marginal or additional costs to doing that job. At worst, my partner and I would have had to work a little harder during that period. The bottom line was that by taking that job, we were made "richer" by the fee we were to receive.

Obviously, you cannot run a business by charging such fees, but it was a one-shot job, it did not disrupt any other work, and it did not change the dynamics of our billing methods. As it turned out, this job was our first job from a very large company, and it led to more work at our standard fees. Eventually, this company became our largest client for a number of years thereafter. And our first inclination was to turn down the work because the fee was so much below our standard rates!

A bottom line question to ask yourself when trying to decide whether to accept a client for a "low" rate fee if you have the available time is how much richer you will be doing the work versus not doing it. Other considerations and practice growth issues exist, but this is one factor to consider.

When I first started my practice, I had an argument with a client over an increased fee, and he said he wasn't coming back. He also multiplied his fee by 20 and told me that was how much revenue he represented and that I was losing out by not having his business over the next 20 years. Thinking about the value of a client in those terms puts a different perspective on it because that was without any fee increases or referrals from him. Then, add the value you would get when you retire and sell your practice.

One more thing no matter how low the fees, you don't get poor from getting checks on a regular basis. As you grow, you can weed out the lower profit clients. Look at the next illustration of the family tree of a tax return client.

Family Tree of a Small Tax Client

Step	Item	Fee
1.	A long-time tax client who you were charging approximately $1,800 recommends a friend's daughter who is a recent graduate and has just started her first job.	
2.	You take her as a client and charge your minimum fee for an individual tax return. Although she is a college graduate, she never made much money, but she has an interesting job as an administrative assistant to the owner of a manufacturing business that sells direct to consumers through a website and catalog mailings. Your fee doesn't increase for the next four years.	
3.	After four years, your client's boss has been approached to sell his business, and the young lady suggests that you might be able to assist him.	
4.	You agree to meet with him for an initial meeting at no charge. The meeting takes two hours.	
5.	You get job and a check for a retainer.	$ 5,000
6.	You help your client present his business in the best light and offer suggestions on how to price and negotiate the transaction. You bill additionally for your time.	$ 22,300
7.	The business sale closes and you get a success fee.	$ 25,000
8.	The buyer's Big 4 accounting firm doesn't want to audit the financial statement, so you get hired to prepare audited financial statements for the last three years.	$ 36,000
9.	The buyer is acquiring another, but much smaller, company, and the Big 4 accounting firm suggests you audit that company. You quote a fixed fee with one exception—to bill extra if the capital account on the books needs cleaning up.	$ 18,000

(continued)

Step	Item	Fee
10.	You receive an extra fee to clean up capital accounts because there were nine layers of raising capital and nothing was reflected properly on the books, except for the cash that was deposited.	$ 11,000
11.	Additional consent work arises for both companies when the buyer files to go public.	$ 3,000
12.	Total fees collected.	$120,300

P.S. This client also recommended another client to us to do tax consulting and eventually the tax returns and where we collected about $40,000 over three years.

Questions

- Where did the long-term client who recommended the young graduate come from? You should trace that family tree.
- How much additional business might you get in the future because of the contacts and experience you got from the preceding additional work?
- What is the value of that (very) small tax return client to you?

Some Best Practices for a Better Tax Season 23

- Back up your hard drives and data.
- Have all your supplies ordered and a mechanism to reorder before you run out, especially paper and soda.
- Read the software instructions and best practices guides.
- If not already, become paperless.
- Use bar codes if your software permits you to bookmark scanned documents and client information.
- Train before your busy season and supplement the training with effective and deliberate on the job training.
- Take the time to do it right the first time.
- If you let staff shortcut a procedure, they will continue to do so five more times until the procedure is done correctly, even after you have caught and corrected them. This destroys your system.
- If staff see you shortcutting a procedure, they will continue to do so 10 more times and likewise will have your system destroyed.
- Update tax and schedule calendars as soon as you get new information or a new client.
- Provide clients with readable and understandable (that is, user-friendly) summaries of their tax returns and instructions for what they need to do to get them filed and have the taxes paid.
- Answer the phone when the client calls if you are in the office. Your job is to answer your clients' calls, even if the call is at 8:52 P.M.
- A client measures your service by the last phone call not returned, not by the business saving work you did two years ago.
- Never forget that the clients pay your salary—they are your customer—and many other people would love to have that business.
- You are in business. Charge the right fee for your services, and bill it promptly.
- Accept credit card payments.

- Tax returns are not just another number for you to cross off the list when the return is finished. Each return represents a unique person who is relying on you to do the best job you are capable of, and then some.
- Give highest priority to quality control, and make that your line in the sand.
- When you lose a client, give a copy of the letter firing you to each person who worked on that client.
- Have a top side review for every return.
- Reviewers should have advanced training, higher level continuing professional education, or a Master's degree.
- Do not look too busy.
- Act like a business and do some low cost and low effort marketing. Include a promotional insert for one of your client services with each invoice sent to clients.
- You should have an organized and uniform place to put information that comes in piecemeal during the year and a place to include notes and memos of discussions with a client during the year, from one tax season to the next. An example is a house closing statement, a divorce agreement executed during the year, stock option details, cost basis of securities sold, and charity receipts sent during the year.
- You should maintain a permanent folder or file for each client. Examples of what belongs here are copies of designation of beneficiary forms a client might send you, a divorce agreement that was used as part of the preparation process, employment contracts, closing statements of property purchased (after they are used when the return is prepared), trust agreements, and partnership or buy sell agreements.
- Note: you should be careful to let a client know that you are keeping certain copies of their information in case it is needed for their tax preparation, an audit or future planning but that you are not maintaining calendars of estimated payments for them because that is solely their responsibility. Do not keep the original documents. You should scan what the clients provide into your digital paperless system and return the originals to them.

It's Supposed to Get Better 24

Tax season is supposed to get better each year. By buying and reading this book and using it as a resource, you recognize that tax season can be better. Hopefully by following some of my ideas and suggestions, it will get better for you.

Here are five things that should be done to make tax season (and the rest of your practice or any business) better:

Training. Training should be in the areas staff will work in and issues they will likely encounter. A thorough post-tax-season review will uncover many of these areas. Many continuing education courses cover generic topics that are not usually specific to the issues staff encounter.

Systems. Procedures, systems, and checklists need to accommodate what actually needs to be done, and they need to be followed. Many firms shortcut procedures in the heat of the moment. If that is permitted, then why not change the standard procedures to what is actually being done? If that is not acceptable, then why are you permitting shortcuts?

Preplanning and scheduling. Tax season is a massive undertaking and needs advance planning and proper work and staff scheduling. Examples are to have staff that worked on a client's return last year scheduled for this year; research difficult issues before tax season begins by more experienced staff; schedule clients with voluminous transactions early in the season or even in December to get a head start, and to time a return's completion with the reviewer so efficient quality control methods can be employed.

Communication. This means that everyone working on a client knows what everyone else working on that client knows. Partners learning things during the year need to transmit this so the people working on the return including the reviewer have access to it, and that the firm's procedures require looking for it. No shortcuts! There also has to be an open line of communication with the client to keep him or her informed of any delays or surprises. Contrarily, clients have to be made aware of the importance of their quick response to requests for additional data and their timely review of what they receive from their accountant.

Buy-In. Tax preparation is a very serious undertaking and the four aforementioned areas need to be implemented with a resolve that insures the best service possible for the clients and a sane and calm tax season. That requires buy-in by management and the entire staff. The culture of the firm has to be where only the best work done the right way at the right time is acceptable.

It's supposed to get better. Not working toward that end is not growth and progress. You better act to make it better starting now, or you deserve what you get!

I appreciate that you read this book and made it to here. You are welcome to call me with any questions, comments, and suggestions. This book is the result of a collaboration of many practitioners and clients and could not have been written without that help. My email address is emendlowitz@withum.com. Send me an email with a brief idea of the topic and include your phone number so I can call you to discuss. If you want any checklists, templates, or letters illustrated in this book, email me and I'll forward to you. No charge.

Again, thank you.
Ed

Afterword

When we send a client his or her tax return, we are sending, for the few moments when he or she looks at it and signs it, the single most important document in his or her life. We must work on that single most important document with that knowledge and the care and attention that the client expects, deserves, and pays for.

Keep in mind the following:

- No system works without commitment and dedication to the system and its processes.
- Without a strong single system, you will have a separate system for each contributing person.
- The system should serve the long term goals of organization.
- The mindset should be to create fantastic customer experiences with the firm.

I Know You Won't Believe This, But It's True…

- A prospect called me saying that he is looking for a CPA to do his tax returns because he has outgrown his present accountant and the accountant makes errors almost every year. However, he first wants to know where I went to college, whether I have any advanced degrees, how much continuing education I attend each year, how else I stay updated with tax law changes, if I give any speeches or write any articles, whether I can handle complicated returns or just do simple ones, my firm's tax return review procedures, and whether I can provide suitable references. After I satisfactorily answer all the questions, I then discuss my fees and billing arrangements. He becomes aghast that I charge more than the storefront tax preparer he has been using for the last eight years.

- Many clients meticulously fill out an organizer that we send at the beginning of each year. However, when they get their completed return, they want us to review every difference with the entries they made on the organizer, which are actually their errors or calculated differences, such as statutory reductions of certain expenses, causing us to spend an extra 30–45 minutes with them. In actuality, it would be easier for us if they just sent us their tax data in an organized manner, skipping the organizer altogether.
- Some clients present themselves in our office with a "shopping bag" full of tax information. Then, they tell us that they are in a hurry because they are already late for their lunch appointment, so they can't go over anything with us, but they would like us to tell them the amount of their refund before they leave.
- A client going on a three week vacation drops off her tax information. While she is away, her daughter mails us nine envelopes with more of her Mom's tax information. When the client returns, she is appalled that we haven't finished her return because she dropped off her information before she left.
- Many clients sell stock they either inherited or received as a gift—sometimes more than four decades ago! When we ask for their tax basis so we can calculate their gain or loss, they tell us they don't know and to "figure something out." We do some limited research, and no matter what we come up with, they tell us they definitely know it wasn't that low.
- Many clients make estimated tax payments during the year. The IRS and state taxing authorities check 100 percent of these amounts that are claimed on the tax returns, and if the amounts don't agree with their records, they send a notice and usually a bill for underpayments, including interest and penalties. Because of this, and to eliminate the inconvenience of the notices, we ask our clients to provide us with proof of their payments. Usually, the clients insist that we should take their word and use the listing they provided us. Those clients who refuse to go through the trouble of providing us the back-up information yell the loudest when they get a notice about us doing the return wrong, even though it was because they wrote down incorrect information on the list they gave us.

- No matter how much we try to explain to clients how they can use our services and benefit the most, many just don't. An example is when a 1-hour meeting is scheduled to get the client's tax information. Some clients come fully organized and prepared and spend approximately 20 minutes showing us what they did and anything new or unusual. They then use the rest of the hour going through a list of tax and financial planning questions designed to make their financial lives more secure and themselves wealthier. Needless to say, they are getting more than they are paying for and the full value of our expertise. However, many clients show up with a pile of papers and sit facing us while opening each envelope and trying to decide if this is something they should give us for their tax return or something they should have paid four months earlier. In some measure, they are wasting what could be a valuable asset and resource for them.
- We have a client who writes "final" on every return he files because that is the final return he is filing for that year. We found this out when he started getting notices asking why he filed a new return when the last return was marked "final." Note that when the IRS receives a final return, they take you off their mailing list.
- A client wrote to the IRS asking to be taken off their mailing list because he no longer wanted to pay taxes.
- We have a client who tried preparing his own return one year; however, the return was rejected because he followed the previous year's amended return: Form 1040X. The IRS said he needed to file a return for the current year and wait at least until after the April 15 due date to file an amended return.
- Some of our clients who receive their completed returns from us in the mail meticulously remove every paper clip and put the returns in one pile, the instructions in another, and the envelopes to mail the returns in another. Then, they call us to ask what to do and where to mail the returns.
- Twenty-five years ago, a client's 94-year-old father spent a day preparing his tax information. The next morning, he went to the post office to mail it to me. That afternoon, he called his son to complain that he sent me his tax information and hadn't yet received his completed return. Well, it is 25 years later, and the son who is

now 94 years old just did the same thing: calling wanting to know why he hasn't received his completed return. The envelope arrived 2 days after that call. Actually, he didn't remember any of it, so he wasn't mad that the return wasn't quickly sent to him.

- Failure to file syndrome has been used as a defense in court to excuse the failure to file multiple years' tax returns. Actually, in a book I wrote in 1984, I had a chapter titled "Fear of Filing" that diagnosed this problem and explained how to handle it to get back in the system.
- I had a client show up one day who had not filed her return for many years, and I told her what I needed to be able to prepare her delinquent returns. When she returned, I started asking her a battery of probing questions, and after a while of listening and responding, she replied, "Seeing you is worse than seeing my shrink, and here I am more revealing!"